AFRICA

My First Missions Trip ...
What Could Go Wrong?

ENDORSEMENTS

"I have known Matt Swiatkowski for more than 20 years. Our odd senses of humor and our shared faith in Christ has given us things to bond over and has turned us into good friends. We, as preachers, are a prideful lot, and while we may be quick to point out the shortcomings of others, we generally try to avoid talking about our own. Pastor Swiatkowski's personality comes through the pages of this book. As he shares some of the unflattering, inner struggles he experienced during his adventure, you feel like you are on the emotional rollercoaster with him. When you finish his book, you find that you have learned much about faith and trusting God through the difficulties of life."

-Dr. David F. Iseminger
Spiritual Care Coordinator Heart to Heart Hospice Flint, MI

"Sitting and reading this book has allowed me to hear, smell, and see West Africa again. As I read, I wept, laughed, and thanked God that I have had the wonderful blessing of visiting Sierra Leone. Pastor Matt's humorous view of his first trip makes this book interesting as well as enjoyable. After reading his account of the mission trip, you may possibly ask, 'Can all of this happen to one man on one trip?' Trust me, it can and does."

-Dr. Steve Ware
Pastor, Tabernacle Baptist Church, Orlando FL

"I must confess, when Brother Matt first asked me to read his manuscript, I was a little hesitant. During the school year, I am pretty busy teaching and, this year, I was even taking a couple of graduate classes. But, Pastor Swiatkowski is a dear friend, and I don't think I could say no to him.

I thoroughly enjoyed reading the story of his trip to Africa. In fact, once I started reading, I could not put it down. I felt as though I was there on the trip with him experiencing the frustrations of cancelled flights and lost luggage, along with the anxiety of not having all of the things that would be needed for the trip: including his sermon notes. But more importantly, I experienced, through his book, the blessings of meeting so many wonderful brothers and sisters in Christ while exploring a very beautiful, yet war-torn and impoverished, land. It was amazing to see God meet every one of his needs and show Himself faithful to Matt along the journey.

As is very typical with anything Matt does, there is a lot of humor in this book. I almost fell off my chair from laughter when I read about Matt's description of the man on the plane next to him on his return flight who had a goat under his jacket. . . or at least smelled like it. Additionally, there is a lot of practical spiritual applications woven throughout the book. Through Matt's "Take Note Swiatkowski" sections, God taught me the same life lessons that He taught Matt on the trip.

This is a very enjoyable read, and I highly recommend it! I have never desired to make a trip like this - until now. I will be looking for an opportunity to visit the mission field in the near future."

-Pastor Phil Erickson
Jersey Shore Baptist Church, Galloway NJ

"With a unique sense of humor and the excitement of a kid on Christmas, brother Matt recounts his first missions trip to Sierra Leone, West Africa. As I read through this book, fond memories flooded back of my first missions trip some years ago. With these memories came the renewed importance that every believer, at some in their life, go on a mission's trip. Throughout the pages of his book, we see the continuing provision of our Heavenly Father in the everyday things of life. Not only are we reminded once again of how truly blessed we are to live in this wonderful country of America, but we are also reminded of the ever increasing need to shine the light of the gospel in this darkened world. I truly enjoyed this read."

-Pastor Brian Phalon
Faith Baptist Church, Sparta NJ

I highly recommend Matt Swiatkowski's book for anyone who loves missions and has an interest in what it would be like to visit a mission field. Prepare to travel on a spiritual journey as you read this amazing account of his first missions trip. You will also learn of God's amazing provision when we seek to serve God by serving others.

-DR. DON WOODARD
Beacon Baptist Church, Salem VA

AFRICA

My First Missions Trip . . .
What Could Go Wrong?

A Journey in Learning to Trust God
through Mishaps and Trials

MATTHEW B. SWIATKOWSKI SR.

AMBASSADOR INTERNATIONAL
GREENVILLE, SOUTH CAROLINA & BELFAST, NORTHERN IRELAND
www.ambassador-international.com

Africa: My First Missions Trip ... What Could Go Wrong?

A Journey in Learning to Trust God through Mishaps and Trials

©2020 by Matthew B. Swiatkowski Sr.
All rights reserved

ISBN: 978-1-62020-976-9
eISBN: 978-1-62020-719-2

Edited by Bethany McDaris
eBook Conversion by Anna Riebe Raats

Unless otherwise indicated, Bible quotations are taken from the King James Version, The Authorized Version. Public Domain.

AMBASSADOR INTERNATIONAL
Emerald House
411 University Ridge, Suite B14
Greenville, SC 29601, USA
www.ambassador-international.com

AMBASSADOR BOOKS
The Mount
2 Woodstock Link
Belfast, BT6 8DD, Northern Ireland, UK
www.ambassadormedia.co.uk

The colophon is a trademark of Ambassador, a Christian publishing company.

For Renee

CONTENTS

FOREWORD

It is with sheer delight, and privilege on my part, that you have asked me to preface your book.

Having personally experienced this missions trip, your book took on a special meaning and conjured up moments that were all but lost to my memory.

Thank you for your unique way of expressing your thoughts and causing reflection.

I believe, the greatest impact of your story was that even though I knew most of the unfolding events, I failed to understand the deep feelings, both of frustration and fear, that you were experiencing. Perhaps God was allowing you to go through these experiences not to hurt you but to deepen your faith and confidence in Him.

Again, thank you for the memories. I am sure your readers will appreciate them as well. Thank you for your gift of humor (which I have always found so refreshing) and for your mind to intrigue others.

Yours for Jesus,

Dr. David Arnold

INTRODUCTION

I HOLD NO VISIONS OF grandeur concerning myself. I do not envision myself as David Livingstone or any other great missionary. I did not go where no white man had gone before, nor did I suffer through disease and fear of death. I did not preach to untold thousands or lead tens of thousands to Christ. I was simply invited to go on a trip to Sierra Leone to be a helper. I was being Timothy to Paul, and my job was to make sure that Brother Arnold was well taken care of. But unknown to me, God would provide opportunities to preach, lead people to Christ, and see places I had never seen before.

This trip is about God teaching me and helping my faith grow.

I am no Superman.

In fact, God has no Supermen. He just has humble servants who need His strength and help every minute of the day. Jesus said, "Without me ye can do nothing" (John 15:5).

I learned this lesson.

I had never been on a missions trip before Africa to any country even though I had been in the ministry since I was eighteen and a pastor for fifteen years. I had been busy in my work as a pastor and raising my family. I am also of the opinion that, as a man, my first responsibility is to my family. After all, I married my wife so I could be with her and so we could serve the Lord together. I did not want to spend weeks away from her and our children time after time.

Like any pastor, I have felt the inadequacies of my abilities, but with the Lord's help, I have grown and learned to trust Him for my needs. Going on a missions trip was no big deal as I would be with men who had done this for countless years and been through many trials. My story is one of humor, of watching God work, and of seeing my faith increase.

I have included sections labeled "Take note Swiatkowski." I don't know when I started doing this, but for many years (when I learn a lesson through my experience or someone else's), I will say to myself, "Take note Swiatkowski."

This is my little reminder not to forget a simple life lesson.

I trust and pray my story will encourage you in your walk of faith, and I hope you realize that the God we serve is able to help you wherever you are.

Chapter One

THE BEGINNING

"Yeah, I'll go."

These were the words that came out of my mouth as we sat in Tops Diner after Sunday night church. This was in response to the question, "Will you go to Africa with me?"

After I gave my answer, Brother Arnold looked at me with a smile.

"Amen," he said enthusiastically.

It was January, and the trip was planned for March. No one was going with Brother Arnold. His wife and daughter were afraid for him to go by himself, so they wanted me to accompany him. I always wanted to go, but I never had the money or the time. I pastored a church, had a wife, and had four children. Any "extra" money went to necessities. . . which means there was never any extra.

Now, I had committed to going, but how could I obtain the money and a passport in time to make the trip?

God has a way of taking our small faith and expanding it. Through this process, I learned that God is all sufficient and that the souls that lean on Him will find all they need.

Before taking this trip, some young ladies at church gave me a beautiful leather journal. My thoughts when I received it were, *"Well, this is nice, but I have no need for such things. I don't write in journals."*

Even through this gift, God was working, but I, in my ignorance, was completely unaware of it. Very soon, I would place the journal in my carry-on bag and make daily entries into it. The notes I took, and the dates, helped me remember all that transpired, and the photographs I took aided me in remembering all the details.

I looked over at my dear wife. The look on her face was one of shock, and I knew there would be a discussion when we returned home. I went back to looking at my plate and thinking to myself, *"What did I just say?"*

But I felt a sense of peace, even excitement, so I didn't think about it for the rest of the evening.

***

Evangelist David Arnold had been coming to our church for several years, and he always asked me to go to Africa with him. I have consistently given the same answer: "Let me pray about it."

To be quite honest, I did very little praying. . . very little. He has ministered in Sierra Leone, West Africa since the early 90's. He was there before, and during, the war, and he saw unspeakable crimes that were committed against the good people who live there.

Depending on the source, there are several reasons that there was a war that ravaged the country for ten years. Hollywood and the media say the war was all about diamonds and gold. It was all to feed the rich man's greed (mostly American greed). The people of Sierra Leone say it was Muammar Gaddafi. Gaddafi, the former dictator of Libya, knew about the riches that were there and sought them for his benefit and the advancement of the Muslim faith.

There are some good documentaries concerning the war in Sierra Leone. One is *Cry Freetown* and the other is *Blood Diamonds* (which is not to be confused with the movie made by DiCaprio, but is instead, a good documentation of events). In either case, I did not see where to lay the blame. Each documentary says that Charles Taylor of Liberia sent in men and arms; however, they do not comment on where the arms came from.

The people of Sierra Leone blame Libya and the now dead dictator. There is even evidence that Al Qaeda was involved. In any case, no matter who was responsible, the dear people of this country suffered unspeakable crimes. The rebels went into the countryside and attacked the villages, and then, at the point of a gun, they began to kill and maim. They forced heavy, addictive drugs upon the people, which almost made them mindless killers. If they wanted another fix, they had to kill, rape, and destroy.

This beautiful country, once part of the British Empire with shops and boutiques, was brought to ruin. After ten long years (and the help of the U.N.), the war came to an end. Only God knows all of the atrocities that were committed.

During the time of war, Brother Arnold's ministry was used by God to provide the Gospel, food, and medicine. There were many lives saved by his faithfulness to obey God. World Evangelistic Outreach (WEO) was started by Brother Arnold for the sole purpose of encouraging God's work. He quit the pastorate and left a large church that he built in order to enter a new door that God had opened. WEO started and built churches and schools in Sierra Leone. Thousands of young Africans were educated in these classrooms. Not only were they given a basic education, but they were also taught the life-changing Gospel of Jesus Christ.

Brother Arnold was after me for years to go with him to see the work of the organization and meet the people. For many of these individuals, I heard their names and saw their pictures so often that I felt as though I knew them already.

TAKE NOTE SWIATKOWSKI

"Yea, they spake against God; they said, 'Can God furnish a table in the wilderness?'" (Psalm 78:19).

I often think of Moses and all that he went through, but mostly, I think of what was required to take care of a multitude of people on a daily basis. When you think of how much food and water was needed to provide for all of Israel, its scope is astronomical. But I love the above verse that says, "Can God furnish a table in the wilderness?" God proved to Israel over and over again that He could provide that table.

As Christians, we must ask ourselves the same question. But to take it a step further, we must ask, "Can God take care of me?"

The prevailing attitude among believers is that God will not take care of them. If God is leading us to do something, then He will foot the bill. Moses never once sent out letters begging for finances or pleading for Egypt to send a small donation.

God's work is funded by God.

This does not mean that we should stop giving our tithe to the church, but it does show us that God is able to take care of us when we give.

If a pastor has a large mortgage to pay, he may begin to beg and even shame people into giving. How many people have been hurt because some preacher could talk about nothing but money and had all sorts of gimmicks to guilt people into contributing? I know the false prophets on TV and the internet are infamous for this, but it's bad when a man of God, such as a pastor, feels he must resort to it.

It is so hard to hear men say, "God is doing great things and is moving mightily, but we need your money to help the work."

This is so unscriptural and sad.

Years ago, I read a small biography on George Mueller, and God impacted my heart with the thought that He will provide for His work. The preacher should tell of the work, express there is a need to God's people, and then pray.

God will not fail to provide for His work.

Have you not read that when they needed material for the tabernacle, Moses asked the people to offer freely and of a willing heart? Please read Exodus 35, and see how this verse shows, what I believe is, the pattern for our giving.

God also provided a man with the wisdom to build the tabernacle. God will provide if we follow His way. If it is the will of God, He will work it out. And if God wants it to go under, we have no business keeping it afloat. We need wisdom from God to know the difference. The book of James tells us that we can obtain wisdom from the Lord.

God taught me a truth from His word, a truth that I read time and time again: God will provide for His work.

Chapter Two

WATCHING GOD PROVIDE

"You will need at least $3,500.00 for the trip," Brother Arnold informed me.

The amount would cover our tickets, visas, and expenses while in Africa. It would also leave me with some spending money as well.

We would be in Sierra Leone, Africa, and there would be a cost for accommodations. We would also need a driver and vehicle to transport us. We would also be traveling to Liberia where we would have a revival meeting and a preacher's meeting. We would need a hotel while there for the gatherings. I also needed money for the passport, the medicine, and the vaccinations.

This trip was adding up fast.

$3,500.00. It might as well have been a million dollars, because I didn't have a dime to my name. Where would I get this kind of money? I couldn't touch the income coming in because we needed that to pay our bills. So, where would it come from? Normally, I would be frantic about such things, but I had a peace in my heart that told me the money would come in.

I know many preachers who have gone on missions trips every year, and I often wondered how they could afford it. Some had large churches, but others didn't. So, I never knew how they could afford these trips. All I knew was that my money was tight, but God had provided for my needs all these years. I always felt bad asking the Lord for money for trips like this when there were other needs that my family had or things we could use that money for. But this time, I felt the Lord was in the middle of the situation, and there was a reason for this trip.

The next Sunday, after I had said I would go to Africa, a lady in our church by the name of Nyra handed me an envelope.

"What is this?" I asked her.

"It's from Kim," she responded.

"Kim who?" I thought.

She then explained it was the Kim who drove a long distance to our church. This was the woman who came with her two children: her son, who was mentally handicapped, and her young teenage daughter. Her daughter, after a period of time, came forward and trusted Christ as her Saviour.

I had not seen them for some time, and the reason was simple: they had moved. Long story short, Kim had sold her house, moved south, and wanted to give me a gift. The envelope contained $500.00.

Praise the Lord!

Kim did not donate that money because she knew about Africa. She gave the money because she felt led by God to do something nice for me. God was showing me that He was in it.

Little by little, the money came in from different sources (mostly church people). They started a fund "Send the Pastor to Africa." I didn't initiate this, they did. I was surprised to see all the different people who were making donations because they were excited to help me go to Africa. I was humbled by all of the loving gestures and overwhelmed by the kindness of these dear people. The donations came in quickly, and in time, I had the amount I needed for the trip.

With money in hand, I purchased the tickets, obtained my visas, and applied for my passport. Even the passport came quickly, which was a miracle because I needed it so soon! Chris, a friend at the Post Office, told me she would put a rush on it but could not guarantee that it would arrive in time for the trip; however, it did come in time. It's encouraging to know that God can move the US government. Once all of the required documents were prepared, I received all necessary medical shots and medicine. Everything was in place. All that remained was for the day to arrive.

Chapter Three

GOING TO DULLES: PLANES, TRAINS, AUTOMOBILES, AND AIRPORTS

SUNDAY

Planes

My wife, Renee, is an expert when it comes to packing. She gained her experience through all of our family vacations over the years.

When we travelled, we loaded all kinds of goodies, shirts, pants, suits, ties, socks, under garments, personal hygiene products, sermons, handouts, and even all of the chargers for the phones and camera in one large suitcase.

Just to be clear, we never had the money to hop on a plane and visit the different states. Our vacations consisted of loading up the family minivan and driving on the American highways. We have seen a great deal of our country this way.

Before my departure, she dragged out the suitcase from the cubby hole in our bedroom closet to help me pack. There would be two suitcases: the carry-on bag and the large one to check in. For this trip to Africa, I squeezed in six baseball hats to give away to the African preachers: three Mets and three Yankee. I have no idea what possessed me to buy the Yankee hats. I also packed extra shoes and even a sun hat for myself. The carry-on bag had a shirt, two pairs of briefs, reading glasses, and medicine of all kinds ranging from Ibuprofen to Antimalarial.

I was all set and ready to go.

My flight was scheduled for 11:00 am Sunday, March 14th. My flight was on a small commuter plane from Newark, NJ to Dulles International Airport in Virginia. On Friday, March 12th, the Northeast was hit by a massive storm. There was flooding, trees were toppled over, and six people were killed.

In short, it was a bad storm.

Once the storm had passed, I went to the airport early and checked my bag. Security was not too bad. I had two hours to kill, so I stopped by McDonalds, ate a small breakfast, and then slowly made my way to the gate where my plane would leave. This is where my calm, peaceful life took a major twist. The next eight and half hours were filled with panic, lost luggage, crowds, late trains, crowds, slow trains, more crowds, a taxi ride, more crowds, a broken train, running, no crowd, and. . . well, just read on and see.

When I went to check in for my flight, the lady at the counter informed me that all the small plane flights were canceled. I stood there, frozen, not sure what would happen next. I must have looked terrified. She told me to go to the United counter, and they would take care of me.

I quickly ran down to the United Continental Airlines desk to see what they could do for me. There was a line, so I patiently waited. When it was my turn, the lady who worked there was stressed out but kind. I explained that my flight was canceled from Newark, but I had a plane to catch in Dulles that night at 6:30 pm. She explained there were no planes going into DC or Dulles. However, the airline would pay to put me on a train to DC. She told me to go to the baggage claim and wait for my bag to come back. Then I was to go to the train station. She gave me a train voucher, and off I went to find where my bag would be returned.

The train would leave at noon. The time was 10:30 am. When the clock turned to 11:30 am, my bag was still nowhere to be seen. There were big bags, small bags, and bright green bags. There were hundreds of bags. . .just not my bag. I went to the bag desk and explained my situation. They informed me that my bag would not return for two more hours.

I had a decision to make. Did I go ahead to the train and pray my bag caught up with me, or did I wait?

Frustrated, angry, and unsure of how to proceed, I bowed my head and prayed. I needed the Lord to guide me and show me what to do. I felt the best course of action was to head for the train station. I would trust God to take care of my bag, and I would head to DC. After all, it was 11:45 am, and my flight out of Dulles was at 6:30 pm. I needed to put miles between me and Newark.

Trains

I waited.

I called my wife to tell her what was going on. To my surprise, she answered even though she was in children's church. I explained my current situation and told her I would keep her posted. After hanging up the phone, I approached the train desk and happily showed them my free ticket.

"When will the train arrive?" I asked.

Being from Jersey, I expected an attitude from the man, but to my surprise, he looked up quickly with a response.

"The computers are all down, and the train is behind schedule. I have no idea when it will be here. Just wait at the station, and I'll let you know something as soon as I do," he said exasperatedly.

So, I sat down to wait.

As I sat there, I realized that the train was going to DC, but I was going to Dulles. They were at least forty miles apart. I would need a taxi to take me to the airport. I overheard a young couple say they were going to Dulles. I approached them and said that I was going to Dulles as well, but the train only went to DC. I suggested that we could split the cab fare and reach our destination at a cheaper rate. They looked at each other with an expression of distrust, but they agreed.

I continued to sit and wait, but I grew restless. Brother Arnold called me and wanted to know what was going on. I told him my situation, and he said he would pray. He was experiencing no delays. He was in Pennsylvania, and the storm had not hit there.

I was tired of waiting; it was getting late. The time was 1:00 pm, so I had an idea. I would hop on the monorail and go to the car rental agency. Then, I could rent a car and just drive down to Dulles.

Off I went.

First, I called my wife and let her know my intentions. I noticed that my battery was at half power on my phone, but my charger was in the suitcase. At that moment I thought, *"I will be on this trip with no phone! How will I talk to my wife? I can't use Brother Arnold's phone because of the cost."*

I didn't have time to worry about it though.

I got off at the stop and made my way down the stairs. I found that the car rental people were very pleasant... NOT! The car rental lady started yelling.

"No car unless you have a reservation."

Thank you, Miss Chuckle Patch. I appreciate your help (that's the Jersey attitude I referred to earlier). As you can guess, I called my wife back and told her how my car rental plan went down in flames. I had no choice but to get back on the monorail.

I thought to myself, *"With the way things have been working for me today, the train has probably come and gone by now."*

But to my surprise, the crowd was still there. So, I sat and waited. Then, the announcement came!

"Please make your way down to the platform, the train will be here soon."

We all took off. Everyone was asking each other the same questions.

"What platform?"

"Where is this train going?"

At that moment, I realized that it doesn't take much to get a large group of people to amass in a certain area. I felt like livestock headed for the slaughter-house. There we were, all standing and staring down the long track with no train in sight. It was at that moment that Brother Arnold called me.

"Where are you?" he asked.

I told him the situation.

"God love ya," he said. "I don't think you're going to make it."

His words were very reassuring and definitely helped calm my already frazzled nerves.

On the platform nobody (and I mean nobody) had a clue. Some stood there trying to be calm while others walked around asking questions that no one had the answers to. When a frantic person asked questions to a calm person, they either gave a vague answer or turned away and pretended they didn't hear anything.

Then, there were people like me. We had no clue, and when asked, we said, "We have no clue."

When we were quizzed some more, we said, "We're here for the ride."

And oh, what a ride it would be.

I called my wife and told her the train was pulling in, and I was getting on it.

"Do you think you should wait?" she asked.

"No," I replied. "I think the Lord is in this, and I should go."

I had the attitude that one can only get so lost, and no matter where I ended up, I could always get back home easily. This was a new outlook for me. I usually played things safe and didn't take too many risks. But a new spirit, or should I say the Holy Spirit, was leading and providing me with boldness.

The Ride

The train pulled in, and I quickly ran to grab a seat in the aisle. There was a young man sitting next to the window. The car was very crowded, and I was glad to have grabbed a seat. I looked around at all those who were standing and noticed that they were all men. If there would have been a lady present, I (most likely) would have given up my seat... maybe.

"By the way," I said to the fella next to me, "Where's this train going?"

"Philadelphia," he said.

I thought to myself, *"Of all the places for a NY Giant fan to end up..."*

"But DC will be the final stop," he said, interrupting my revelry.

"How many stops will there be?" I asked.

"Trenton, Philly, Baltimore, and then DC," he replied.

The conductor walked by, and I asked him what time we would arrive in DC.

"I have no idea! We are already an hour and half behind schedule!" He retorted.

He quickly moved on, and I thought, *"Thank you, kind sir. Based on your response, you must be married to the lady who worked at the car rental place."*

As the train was going down the track, I thought that I would never make it to Dulles on time. My fears were based on the fact that the cars on the side streets were going faster than we were. Yep, the train I was on seemed to be just a little slow. But, as we proceeded down the tracks, we picked up speed which was a relief.

I struck up a conversation with the young man next to me. He was well dressed, and so, I asked what he did for a living.

"I work for Michael Jordan," was his response.

"Really?" I asked.

Why do we say things like that to people when they give us an answer?

"Yes," he said. "What do you do?"

"I'm a Baptist preacher."

"Really?" he said.

We had a pleasant conversation. He later told me that he was a Christian. We made it into Philly, and he departed. No sooner did he vacate the seat than another young man sprang into it. The train was packed to the gills. The young man next to me said he rode the train every weekend and it was never like this.

I noticed a young lady moving through the crowd while looking at me the entire time. I thought to myself, *"What does she want? Probably my seat."*

Then I realized that it was the lady from the train station who I approached about splitting cab fare earlier that day.

"Are you still interested in splitting the cab fare?" she asked once she reached me.

"Sure! Once we make it to DC, we can meet up on the train platform," I responded.

How she made her way through the cars and found me was another small miracle.

After the arrangements were made, I struck up a nice conversation with the young man next to me. I told him of my trip, how I was going to Africa where I would preach, and how I would try to be a blessing. He said he was a Christian as well, and we enjoyed our time together.

As I was sitting there, I had begun to go into deep thought about everything that had happened. My body was in a crowded train, but my mind was a million miles away thinking and beginning to stress out.

The Bible says that Satan is a liar, and we must always believe this fact. As I sat on the train, the continual thoughts going through my head were that I wouldn't make it in time, that I would miss my flight, and that I would then be stranded in Dulles. This last bit did not bother me though. I could always rent a car (after securing a reservation) and just drive home. Because, even if I could catch a later flight to Brussels, there were only so many flights to Freetown, Sierra Leone. If that happened, I would miss a week of Africa. All the money raised would be wasted. People had contributed to help me, and I would miss half of the trip.

"God, why would You do this to me?" I thought.

I was sure He had led me to go on this trip, and now, it seemed that He would let me miss half of it. It was bad enough that I had no luggage, and I didn't know if it would ever get to Africa. I knew that it wasn't good to let things like this fester in my mind, and yet, there I was. I knew that the doubt was not of God, but I was fearful of what would happen even as I tried to remember that God was not the author of my fear.

While sitting on the train in the midst of the chaos and my fear, I had a strange sensation come over me. I bowed my head and prayed.

"Lord, will I make my flight tonight?"

"Yes, Matt. You will make your flight," I heard the Holy Spirit speak to my heart just as surely as I was on that train.

It was as clear that the thought came from God as the voice of the man next to me. I do not expect those who are not Christians to understand this revelation, but it was real. In that moment, I was overwhelmed with joy, love, and gratitude to my Savior. God had spoken to my heart, and the Spirit of God had filled and flooded me with His peace and assurance. With people on every side of me, the Lord and I had enjoyed fellowship.

I decided to pray again. I don't know why I asked the Lord what I did, but I felt like I had the liberty to do so.

"Lord," I began, "will I be the last one on the plane?"

"Yes, Matt. You will be the last one," He sweetly responded.

I sat there with tears running down my cheeks as I tried to hold back my emotion. I had wanted to shout and weep at the same time. God was so good to me, and I surely did not deserve such kindness. I told the Lord thank you. I had a peace knowing that God was in control. If God was for me, then who could be against me?

The answer was simple: no one.

I now knew how the Apostle Paul must have felt when the Lord came to him and assured him that he would be safe as he was tossed about on the ocean in Acts 27. I'm no Paul, but I serve the same God he did.

As the train pulled into DC, I had been filled with a new sense of confidence. I said goodbye to the young man who had sat next to me thinking that I would never see him again. Then, we all began the mad rush down the platform and up the stairs to the taxis.

Automobiles

"You have got to be kidding me."

This was my first thought when I looked at the line of people that had to be at least fifty yards long. That was how many people were in line waiting for taxis. The time was now 5:00 pm, and my flight would leave at 6:30 pm.

At that moment, Brother Arnold called me again to ask where I was.

"I'm at Union Station now, and I'm trying to get a cab to Dulles."

"God love ya, Matt! You're a world traveler," he responded.

No, I was just a guy watching God part the Red sea, that was all.

This was my first time in Union Station, and I could honestly say that, just as Mr. Smith (Jimmy Stewart) saw the Capitol from the inside of this place, I also saw it; however, I did not have time to get excited about it. Despite the fact that all I needed was a taxi, the line was a good half hour wait.

I almost went into panic mode again when I looked to the front of the line and saw the young man I had sat beside on the train from Philly to DC. He was third in line. I looked at him, and he looked at me at the same time. With just a little nod of his head, he was telling me to join him in line. Now, I felt bad doing that because of the people waiting, but I quickly got over my emotions. In fact, I beat it to death with a mental stick and took my place in line. I think there was some grumbling, but I blocked it out. I shook his hand, said thank you, and told him I appreciated his kindness.

It was my turn for a taxi. No sooner had the cab driver summoned me than I saw the young couple who was supposed to split cab fare with me.

I waved at them.

They came running, and we all jumped into the cab together.

"Where're you going?" the cabbie asked.

"Dulles," I said. "I'm in a hurry, so don't spare the gas pedal."

He smiled, and we proceeded on our way.

There comes a time when you realize your age and how even ten years can make such a difference. As we were leaving DC, we drove past Fort Marcy Park.

"Hey, that's where they found Vince Foster," I said.

"Who?" they asked.

I looked at the young couple and realized they would have been kids in early grammar school when the event I mentioned had taken place. I shook my head.

"It's not important."

They went back to snuggling in the back seat of the taxi. I began to realize just how much older I was getting and how much life experience I had over most people. These truths will help an individual be a better person as well as being a better person for the Lord.

There was no traffic to speak of, and we made good time to the airport. The young couple had been nice. I was able tell them of my trip up to that point and how good God had been to me. They were not as concerned about the time as I was because their flight was not until much later that evening.

I asked how much the taxi fare was, quickly tossed them my money with a tip, and then went on my way.

The Airport

I made it.

It was 5:45 pm, and I had 45 minutes to spare. I ran inside. Since I had no bag to check, I went to the Kiosk, grabbed my ticket, and ran towards the gate.

As I approached security, I looked at the long line of people trying to get through the Transportation Security Administration. What would we do without the TSA? I don't want to sound grumpy, but at that point of the trip, my patience was running thin. There was no doubt that at least 200 people were trying to pass through security.

I tried to call Brother Arnold, but the airport was a dead zone. I couldn't reach him to tell him I was in the airport. I wanted to ask him to please hold the plane. I had seen earlier that the flight was on time, so I did not have a second to spare.

There I stood, waiting. . . again.

Then, for some unexplained reason, they closed a security checkpoint and funneled us all into two lines. Why did they do this? I had no idea, but I thought to myself, *"If this is government efficiency at its best, I can't wait until they control health care."*

Slowly, step by step and inch by inch, we made our way through the metal detector. These were Harry Potter wannabes with the "magic wands" they scanned us with. I was now on the other side, and I just had to get to my gate. It was 6:20 pm, and all I needed do was hop on the monorail. I ran to where I needed to be and stood there waiting for the train. This seemed all too familiar, but hey, at least these things came every minute. So, I should have been on one in no time.

"Here it comes," I said.

It sure was moving super slow. It crawled into the station, the doors opened, we all shoved on board, and the doors closed. There we stood as the train slowly began to limp away. It was déjà vu all over again. As I looked out the monorail window, the lady in the terminal using a walker was going faster than we were.

Then an announcement came.

"This train is out of service. Please exit the monorail and wait for the next car."

The next car arrived, and it quickly took me to the terminal where my gate was located.

There was once a day when I was quite the sprinter, and very few could catch me. The doors opened, and I began to run. I thought, *"This isn't too bad, you still have it Swiatkowski."*

I turned a corner and there was a long hallway. For fear of exaggerating, I won't say how long. But the next year, when I would make a return trip and walk the same tunnel, I said to myself, *"This is a long hallway."*

I continued to run.

The 40 extra pounds that I carried on a daily basis began to slow me down. Personally, I don't believe it's a good thing when you grab your side and suck in air like it may be your last. So, I decided to walk.

I made it to the escalator.

It was then that I noticed, everyone who I had run past, was now walking past me. Up the escalator I went. I reached the top and looked at the signs to see if I should go right or left to my gate. It was to the right. In fact, it was the first gate I came to. I looked up at the gate number and then at the gate area. My heart sank as I looked around. The gate area was empty. The only person there was a man wearing the jackets you see from the workers on the runway. You know, a black jacket with yellow fluorescent stripes on it. I stood there sweating and out of breath.

"Did the plane leave?" I managed to ask between pants for air.

He looked up and stared at me.

"One second," he said as he disappeared behind the door that lead to the plane.

I stood there for what seemed like forever just waiting. Finally, the door opened wide. Several stewardesses came out. I think they're called flight attendants now, so please forgive me. I honestly didn't care what you called them; I was glad to see them. They didn't seem very happy, but it didn't matter. I was happy.

"You must be the man who has friends waiting for him," they said.

"I guess I am," I said as I shrugged.

I wasn't really sure what they meant, but I told them I had been stuck in the airport for the last hour trying to get to the plane. They didn't seem to care about my tale of woe. I made my way inside the plane and walked through First Class. I had a big smirk on my face, but I only received angry glares from the people in their spacious, comfy lounge chairs. One guy in particular was outraged, but I didn't care. I had a smile that went from ear to ear, so I gave him a wink as I walked by. I made my way past the First Class grumps to find my seat. I noticed that the people in the cheap seats weren't too happy with me either, but c'est la vie.

As I walked back to my seat, Brother Arnold looked up and saw me coming. He jumped up and grabbed me.

"Praise God!" he yelled.

There were two other men who were traveling with us. Once we arrived in Africa, we would part ways after the first two days.

People on the plane began to stare with all three men jumping up and yelling, "Praise God!"

We hugged and laughed. We were told to find our seats because the plane needed to taxi out to the runway. *"Yes, praise God,"* I thought. It was then that I remembered what the Lord had said to me on the train ride.

"Yes, Matt. You will be the last one on the plane."

Yes, I was! I choked up with emotion and tears coming down my face as I thought of how God had taken care of me.

TAKE NOTE SWIATKOWSKI

"The steps of a good man are ordered by the LORD: and he delighteth in his way" (Psalm 37:23).

We have often heard the expression, "God's train is never late," but I don't think this was God's train. If it was, there would have been seats for everybody on it; however, I do believe God is in control, and He guides His followers. God directed my path, and I needed to learn to trust His Holy Spirit. If God wanted me in Africa, as I believed He did, then I would get to Africa.

The believer must learn that hindrances are not meant to frustrate us and cause us to be irritable, but rather, they are meant to help us watch the hand of God move. I had often preached that we needed to trust God, and now, God would make me practice what I had preached. This was a day I could have used the old expression, "If it can go wrong, it will."

I would like to be able to say, that through everything, I remained cool and calm and never grew frustrated, but I would be lying. It had been a very strange day of emotions. On the one hand, I had been frustrated, but on the other, God led me through and created a peace about me.

Again, I was reminded of what Jesus said, "Oh ye of little faith."

Why did I let myself get frustrated? Why didn't I just believe God and trust His lead? After all, didn't we sing the song, "Anywhere with Jesus, I can safely go"? I mean, I could sing it, but why didn't I practice it? These are questions constantly asked, but they lead to discouragement instead of confidence. Such thoughts must be combated with scripture. The only way to use scripture is if we first make a daily habit of reading and studying the Bible. My Saviour taught me to cast my cares upon Him.

Chapter Four

FIRST TIME ACROSS THE ATLANTIC

Across the Pond to the Old Country

I needed a place for my carry on, but there was no room in the overheads. The attendant took my bag and stored it in First Class. At least part of me was riding in style.

I found my seat. I was tired, sweating, and in need of a restroom. In fact, I had needed one for the last four hours, but there hadn't been time for any such pleasure. I was also dying to take off my shoes because my feet were sore and hot, but I thought this might not be a good idea. I was sitting next to a stranger, and we had a long flight ahead. I didn't normally have a problem with my feet, but this was not a normal day. I did not dare risk causing panic amongst my travel companions.

It's funny how you can get jealous looking at someone with their shoes off. I mean, all around me people were relaxing and kicking off their shoes; one old boy even had slippers on! I would survive and peel them off later.

The travel agency we used did not book our seats side by side, but I wanted to talk to my friends. They sat behind me and across the aisle, so I was still able to chat with them. It was there that they told me how they held up the plane and refused to board till I got there. They really put up a good fight, but when threatened that they would be left behind, they got on board. The airline assured them that they would put me on another flight, and I would be ok.

When the plane was up and in the air, I needed some Aspirin from my carry-on bag. Brother Arnold walked with me, and I told my tale of all that had happened. I opened the little curtain that prevented the peasants from seeing the lifestyle of the rich and famous in First Class and grabbed what I needed from my high-quality Kmart carry-on bag. I've never seen flight attendants move so fast as when the curtain was opened by the bleacher creatures. I explained who I was and grew envious of the moist towels being distributed to refresh the upper-class. I am convinced that it is best we not know what goes on in First Class once they close the mystical curtain.

I made my way to the bathroom, and I splashed cold water on my face once I was inside. I wiped my neck and brow. I then bowed my head in prayer.

"Thank you for taking care of me, Lord. . . but what about my luggage? My clothes, sermons, toiletries, gifts, battery chargers, and all my other necessities are all in there."

God did not respond.

I would just have to wait until I got to Brussels and see what the airline could do for me.

The men who were traveling with us were Lee Weaver and Pastor Richard Noggle. Lee was a farmer from Pennsylvania. It is through Lee and his dear wife, Peggy, that Dave Arnold was introduced to Sierra Leone. Lee, apart from his farm work, was a missionary involved in drilling water wells in Sierra Leone. Water is scarce, and sometimes, it can be a mile or more that a village has to walk to retrieve it. Lee, with funds raised in America, often went to Africa. With the proper equipment, he dug the wells so there would be clean and safe water for the people. Lee was a fine Christian man who walked with God, and the Lord used him to not only provide physical water, but also to introduce the spiritual water of life. He loved the people of Sierra Leone and risked his life on many occasions (especially during the war).

Brother Arnold and Brother Lee told me stories of running for their lives and hearing gunfire go off as they were ministering. Their stories should be written down and told, but I was not there, and these men should be the ones to tell them. Brother Lee was a good friend, and I enjoyed his company. I was glad to travel with him.

Richard, the man who was with him, was a Methodist preacher of the gospel. I had liked him from the start because he was fun and full of wit. He would have a great deal of wit and humor later on at my expense, but it would all be in good fun. Richard, and his church, supported Lee as a missionary, and he had been invited by Lee to see the work firsthand. It's good for preachers to go out into the field and see what is going on. Then, go back home to tell the people what God is doing. This encourages people to continue contributing to missionary work.

As we settled into our flight, I gazed out the window at the ocean beneath us. How vast and grand it was. I looked for ships that might be passing below, and I believe I saw one. I felt so small as I gazed on the mighty Atlantic Ocean and rested in the truth that my Father put it there. It has been there for thousands of years. Untold millions have sailed it, and many have died in it. I thought of my ancestors who had crossed it leaving Europe for a new life in America, and here was their grandson, or great grandson, flying over it.

It was a lot to take in.

The sun was setting, and I was tired from a long day. I leaned back my chair and tried to sleep. I didn't do well sleeping in a sitting position, so I dozed in and out all night.

MONDAY

The Old World

When I woke up in the morning, the sun was beginning to rise. As I looked out the window, I saw land passing by below us.

"Excuse me," I said to the attendant. "What country am I looking at?"

"It's Ireland," she said. "We'll be passing over England next."

"Wow, Ireland and England! How exciting is this?!" I said to myself.

I couldn't believe I was looking at these sites. My great grandmother came from England, so my roots were there. As I gazed upon the landscape, I thanked my Heavenly Father who allowed me to see this site with all the history involved and the centuries of tales and legends. There was a large city down below. Again, I enquired, and I was told it was London. Then, as we crossed over the English Channel, one other thought had filled my mind: my dad. He had been here during WWII, and I thought of all the brave Americans who fought here to liberate the world from the Nazis.

My God had let me see it, and even though it had been from the air and the dawn hours, my heart was filled with praise and thankfulness.

We landed in Brussels, and as soon as we left the plane, I wanted to find a restroom so that I could change my shirt. It desperately needed changing after all I had been through the previous day. I put on the only other shirt I had: a short-sleeved polo. And low and behold, it was just a little too snug for my liking. Over the winter, sitting in its storage bin, it had shrunk. It couldn't be me that had gained weight. Oh no! It was the lousy storage container's fault for causing it to shrink. I had to keep it on because the other shirt needed a good bath.

"Brother Arnold, do you think this shirt looks too tight?" I asked as I cautiously emerged from the bathroom.

"You look good!" he responded quickly. "God love ya, Matt. You look like a man. I wish I looked like you."

God bless the dear man. I believed he was half senile, but his kind remarks made me feel a little less self-conscious.

I called home so I could talk to my wife and tell her where I was. After giving her the latest update, I asked, "Could you call the airline and ask about my bag?"

"Of course I will," she said.

After saying goodbye, I enquired about my bag at the airline desk in Brussels. After some time, they told me by bag was still in Newark, NJ. They would work on trying to forward it as soon as possible.

We waited in the terminal for a while, then we boarded the Brussels airline to Africa. Once again, I was thrilled to be taking the trip. I was so filled with excitement and joy. My glee could barely be contained much like a child on Christmas morning.

The (Not So) Dark Continent

Without a doubt, this was the friendliest airline I had ever been on. They bent over backwards to try and find my luggage, and the service on the plane was great. We received drinks and snacks, and the meal they served was enormous and delicious. This was a much shorter flight to Africa than the one from Dulles to Brussels, and yet, we were pampered.

This trip provided me a window seat, and I spent most of my time gazing out of the window staring at God's creations. In the distance, I saw what looked like snow-covered mountains, so I asked what they were. The Swiss Alps was the reply. Can you believe it? How beautiful and magnificent they were. I lament that the Lord did not give me the skill of tongue and pen to adequately relay the indescribable sights I saw out that window.

We traveled over France, past Spain, and through northern Africa. I cannot explain the Sahara desert from the air except to say two things: first, its beauty is beyond description. Second, if you don't see God in it, you must be blind. There were browns, pinks, reds, whites, swirls of color, shadows, and rivers cutting through the landscape with their twists and turns on one side and mountain ranges on the other.

As I looked down upon the mountain ranges, one side had one set of colors and the other had a completely different set. I placed my camera against the window and began snapping, but as they say, the pictures don't do them justice. There were ridges in the desert that looked like God, through His omnipotence, took His fingers and scraped them through the rocks. It also looked like it was all washed with a flood and was left to dry.

There was one river that ran straight as an arrow and another next to it that was crooked as a snake. In the middle of nothing, there were (what appeared to be) houses. What could that be? Brown all around for hundreds of miles, and then this little clump of houses.

Gazing at the desert, it looked like brown clouds with blue spots. When I stared too long, I couldn't tell if I was looking up or down. My first thought was that this place had been forsaken by God, but then I looked closer and asked God for understanding. He showed me that the blue I was looking at were valleys. There were black rocks covered with white sand which gave the appearance of snow. The rocks and mountains were flat, yet they had ridges in them as if water was running off of them. I saw all of this and could clearly see the evidence of a flood. No, it was not forsaken by God. No, not at all. My Father had painted and created all of this. He was there, and He is in all of His creation.

We landed at the airport in the city of Conakry in Guinea. Several passengers disembarked while others boarded. We stayed on the plane, and in no time, we were on our way. We soon landed at the airport in Lungi, Sierra Leone. The sky was just turning dark when we arrived, and I could not wait to hop off the plane and set my feet on African soil.

TAKE NOTE SWIATKOWSKI

"Where is God?" the people ask.

Well, I can tell you that I have personally seen the hand of God.

"To the chief Musician, A Psalm of David. The heavens declare the glory of God, and the firmament sheweth his handywork. Day unto day uttereth speech, and night unto night sheweth knowledge. There is no speech nor language where their voice is not heard. Their line is gone out through all the earth, and their words to the end of the world. In them hath he set a tabernacle for the sun" (Psalm 19:1-4).

"He hath made the earth by his power, he hath established the world by his wisdom, and hath stretched out the heavens by his discretion" (Jer. 10:12).

"Because that which may be known of God is manifest in them; for God hath shewed it unto them. For the invisible things of him from the creation of the world are clearly seen, being understood by the things that are made, even his eternal power and Godhead; so that they are without excuse" (Rom. 1:19-20).

How does a man deny the existence of God? I believe, a man must be filled with hate or complete lack of reality. Everything in life demonstrates a designer. From all points of life, we cannot escape it. A book, a computer, a car, everything says I was designed by someone. Yet, when it comes to the creation of us, we throw common sense out the window and say it was the result of time, trial, and error. How foolish can man be?

Obviously, he is very foolish.

I believe some people are mad at God, and so, they strike back with the idea that He doesn't exist. After all, if there is a loving God, why is there so much suffering in the world? And why this and why that? Oh, but friend, God does exist, and He is real. His creations speak His name and point towards His magnificence. Men will deny God exists because if they do acknowledge Him, then they have to believe in accountability, and men fear that. Even the Christian must give an account to God one day, not for sin but for our service. There, we will either have reward or lack of it.

Chapter Five

MY FIRST NIGHT IN AFRICA

First Impressions

When I left New Jersey, it was raining. When I left Dulles, it was raining. When we landed in Brussels, it was raining. Now, in Sierra Leone, I thought it looked like it would rain, but that was just the way it looked in the evening. It was the dry season, and there was hardly any rain that time of year.

The first thing to hit me, upon arrival, was the smell. It was the smell of wood burning. . . a different kind of wood that I had never smelled in the states. A cloud of smoke cradled everything in sight. I realized that here, there were few stoves that used natural gas or propane, and I never even saw an electric stove. All the cooking was done with a fire in some fashion or another. With the high humidity, at times, it caused the smoke to lay low in the air giving the appearance that there might be rain. This assumption, of course, was my first impression. Later, when I adjusted to my surroundings, I realized there was no rain in sight.

At the airport, we walked down the staircase, onto the runway, and into the terminal. I looked up and saw a sign that said Freetown Airport (even though we were in Lungi). We made our way inside, went through customs, and then to the baggage claims area. I didn't have to worry about my bag. . . it was still in Jersey.

A little while later, we were met by Solomon Gorvie. Solomon was a key player in all that took place on my trip, and I grew to love Solomon as a brother.

Solomon was born and raised in Freetown. He loved the Lord and had attended and graduated Bible College in Accra. He had much wisdom and bore many burdens.

His father was Bishop Max Gorvie. The Bishop (as he was called) was a very godly man and was a faithful servant of our Lord, Jesus Christ. Someone needs to write a book on the life of this man and his service for Jesus. What he had done and gone through would put the average American preacher to shame. His wife died years earlier giving birth to their son Theophilus. He was in Bible College in Accra, Ghana during my visit, and I did not get to meet him.

Once all introductions had been made, we proceeded out of the back of the airport terminal to a bus that would take us to the ferry. I was a little fuzzy on why we needed a ferry, but later I understood the geography of it all. By the time we boarded the bus to go to the ferry, the sun had set. All the while, people were asking to help with our luggage simply because they wanted the tip money. These were poor people.

It had never dawned on me that there would be no streetlights. As we made our way through the streets, I remember looking out the window at the people holding the little candles in their hands and seeing the lamp lights in their homes as well. There was something else I could not quite figure out along the road in the pitch black. People were sitting in, what appeared to be, little wooden huts. The only reason I had known they were there was from the small source of light they had. These little booths lined the roads, and I was curious. Unfortunately, Brother Arnold and Solomon were busy talking, and Lee and Richard were in the back. So, I continued to stare out the window in amazement.

This experience was all new to me, and I found it very intriguing.

The Staten Island Ferry, It Is Not

There are several ways to get to Freetown from Lungi. Both of these cities sit on the coast, so you could drive. The map would tell you it takes two hours by car; however, with the roads and congestion, it would be more like six hours. You could take a helicopter. Although it would be fast, it would also be expensive. I never saw the helicopter, but from the description, it sounded like a Vietnam leftover. They said there was a big nut that held the blades in position. They all called that nut "Jesus" because they prayed to it asking it to stay in place. You could take the water taxi, which was a speed boat equipped to carry passengers and was quite fast. Or, you could take the ferry. This final choice was our mode of transportation. It was now 9:00 pm.

When we approached the dock where the ferry was, Solomon asked me for my valuables. He was going to put them in his backpack and hold them for me. He said there would be bad people on the boat, and they would pick-pocket me or just take my valuables from me. I was a little reluctant to relinquish my stuff as I had wanted to take pictures on the ferry, but afterwards, I realized he had been right. It would not have been a good idea to hold onto everything myself. I learned, as the trip went on, that people stole simply because they were hungry. It was a popular belief that if you were white, you had money because you had come to Sierra Leone for diamonds or gold.

The ferry was an old boat. If it had been in the states, OSHA would have decommissioned it in a heartbeat. Solomon had bought first class tickets, and I was excited to sit in first class. That is, until I saw first class. It was a large room with folding chairs and benches, a wooden counter where you could purchase snacks and a cold drink, and an old television suspended from the ceiling playing music videos very loudly. I was surprised to see that the videos were African artists singing gospel songs. One song in particular seemed to be a fan favorite. It was a young lady singing a catchy little tune. I could not make out what exactly she was saying because of the accent, but it sounded like she was saying "My God is Sony."

"That can't be right," I thought.

After several loops, I figured out that she was saying, "My God has done it," but with the accent, it sounded more like "My Gawd has dawn it."

I found myself sitting in first class, surrounded by a whole host of interesting people, clutching my carry-on bag while singing this song. In fact, when I returned the next year, we had three other men with us (two of whom were preachers), and this song still seemed to be number one on the hit list. They had the same problem I did in trying to figure out what she was saying. I was sitting in the back of our van, and the driver had a CD playing. This song came on, and all the preachers were singing and bee bopping to the tune. I recorded it and chuckle whenever I see it.

Back on the ferry, Brother Arnold wanted to talk to Solomon and get some fresh air, so we all went top side, stood on the open deck, and left first class behind. It was there that I saw some of the saddest looking people in my life. We were the only white people on the ferry. In Africa, it is a common thing for them to yell out to you, "Hey, white man."

There is no slur involved because, to them, they are simply stating the obvious. They have not been conditioned with political correctness.

When I studied the people on the ferry, they were all very tired looking as mothers held babies, young men sat staring into nothing, and others gazed at me with obvious envy thinking that I was a rich American or European. Some of them looked at me with a dead stare, and it was a little spooky. But no matter who it was, old and young, male and female, the ride was quiet with no laughing or joking around. There was the sound of babies crying, but even the young people were not playing or running. To add to the eeriness, the deck was very poorly lit, in fact, it was very dim.

"This is the saddest group of people I have ever been around," I thought.

We made our way across the ocean and began to see the light of Freetown in the distance. I remember trying to figure out what I was looking at. It was pitch black, and there were only a few stars visible because of the humidity and clouds. At first, it looked like there was light coming from small skyscrapers when only a few of the lights are on in the tall buildings and they are scattered from floor to floor. After all, this was the capital city, so there must be a skyscraper or two. However, this was not the case. There were no skyscrapers in Freetown. So, what was I looking at? What were those lights so high up in the air?

As we got closer (this was a two-hour ride keep in mind), everything came into focus. Freetown was a city on a mountain; in fact, the name Sierra Leone is a Portuguese word that means Lion Mountain. The lights I had seen were from different homes scattered all along the mountainside, and from a distance at night with no depth perception, they looked like tall buildings.

We made it to Freetown, and we all disembarked. Solomon had a car waiting for us. Lee and Richard had their own car. Lee and his wife had a young man there that they have now adopted as their son, Brima, and he took Lee and Richard to where we were all staying.

Through the Streets At Night

When I got into the car, I tried to use my cell phone to call home to tell my wife I had arrived. It's a good thing that, before I left the states, I contacted my phone carrier and told them of my trip. They informed me that I would need another phone for this occasion, and they would ship it to me. Before I left, I was to activate it so that I would be all set. Well, so much for that! The phone would not work even though Sierra Leone was on the list of countries they said it would work in.

Frustrated, I borrowed Brother Arnold's phone and called home. There was a four-hour time difference, so what was around 11:00 pm to me was 7:00 pm back home. I did not want to run up the bill for Brother Arnold, so our conversation was brief. She told me that I needed to go to the Brussels airline office in Freetown to talk with them as soon as I could.

We started towards where we were going to stay, and I was fascinated by what I saw as I looked out the window. People were everywhere. They were walking the streets up and down the side of the mountain. Hundreds of people just walking. There was very little lighting as only some of the homes had lights, but even those were very dim. Again, I saw the little wooden booths with a candle in them. I asked Solomon what they were.

"Those are stores," he said.

"*Stores?*" I thought.

I turned to him in confusion.

"What do you mean they're stores?"

"They sell things there," he informed me.

I did not understand, nor would I, until the next day in the light. To be honest, I was too exhausted at that moment to comprehend what he was saying. I had slept some on the plane, but it wasn't much. To add to this, I had found the whole drive at night a little frightening. . . mostly because it was a strange place. But, as time went on, I felt right at home there.

Finally, we arrived at our destination. I was very relieved to be there. It was a sense of joy and "Yes, I made it!"

We pulled into a large driveway, proceeded for a few yards, and then turned through a gate and into a courtyard.

Be It Ever So Humble . . .

Our home, for the next few days, was owned by the Catholic Church. It was a Mission in an area called Kingtom. That's right, Kingtom. . . not Kingdom. It is found in Freetown on the northern part. They rented to all comers; it didn't matter who you were. It can be found on Google Earth right beside White Man's Bay (yes, that's the correct name, too).

After securing our room from the office, we grabbed our bags and made our way down the outside hallway to the place of our residence. The entire complex was all one story and was spread out over several acres. Our chamber was a large room with some comfortable chairs, a couch, and a small table to eat at. On the left side of the room, there were two bedrooms. In the center back of the room, the bathroom. And to the right of the bathroom, one bedroom.

Solomon's wife, Matilda, prepared a meal for us, and we enjoyed the fried fish, french fries, and bottled water. We talked and ate for an hour, and then, finally, it was time for bed. Brother Arnold, Richard, and I stayed in the larger chamber with the adjoining rooms while Lee had a smaller room to himself down the hall.

My room had a desk and chair, a dresser, and a bed with mosquito netting hanging from the ceiling surrounding it. It also had a set of windows with bars on them and a ductless A.C. unit which kept the room nice and cool.

Without my luggage, I had no toothpaste or toothbrush. So, I borrowed some toothpaste and used my finger to brush my teeth. It may sound uncivilized, but it worked. I unpacked all of my belongings, and trust me when I say, it wasn't much. The one dilemma I had was where to hide my cash? This was a country that, at the time, did not use credit cards, so cash was needed for transactions. With no good place to hide it, I placed it in my socks and put it in the drawer.

That was my dad's hiding place. When he passed away, my brother and I had to go through all of his socks and underwear to check for money.

Once in my room, I sat down and kicked off my deck shoes. I cannot describe the relief of this dear moment in time. It was 12:30 am on Tuesday. I had worn those shoes since Sunday morning and had been on three continents. There was a vast amount of steam that rose from my feet and a delighted cry of exhalation on my part.

As I sat there rubbing my sore, tired, hot feet, I reflected on all that had transpired. It had been a long two days, but I was safe and sound in Africa. God was so good to me. In my carry-on bag, my dear wife had packed a pair of shorts, so I slipped them on and crawled into bed. I put my mosquito netting in place. I was excited to sleep with mosquito netting.

"Wow! This is real life African stuff going on here," I thought to myself.

With my netting in place, I laid down and proceeded to slip into a much-needed coma like sleep. I have always been able to fall asleep quickly, but this was record time. In fact, I don't even remember putting my head on the pillow.

TAKE NOTE SWIATKOWSKI

"It is vain for you to rise up early, to sit up late, to eat the bread of sorrows: for so he giveth his beloved sleep" (Psalm 127:2).

"I will both lay me down in peace, and sleep: for thou, LORD, only makest me dwell in safety" (Psalm 4:8).

What a wonderful Bible truth that the Lord who created the world also designed it, and us, to rest and sleep. This is where the body reenergizes, and it is here that the child of God should learn to pray and ask the Father to guard them. We should ask for protection from the things of the world and from the enemy.

Whether remembered or not, everyone dreams. Sometimes, dreams can be evil . . . even nightmares plague the child of God. We should learn to pray and humbly ask the Father to provide us with sweet dreams. It would also help if we stopped filling our mind, throughout the day, with bad images and the like.

The Lord can give you perfect rest. Even if it is a short night, He can multiply it so that four hours may have felt more like eight.

I had gone to sleep in a faraway place filled with strangers. I was in a country still filled with those who had murdered and maimed their own citizens; however, I was at rest. I did not have even one ounce of fear.

God sure was good to me.

Chapter Six

AFRICA AT LAST

TUESDAY

Godless Roosters and Government

I was in a deep, deep sleep when I began to stir because of an unusual sound I did not expect.

A rooster was crowing.

"This can't be happening. . . What time is it? I thought these creatures only crow when the sun comes up," I thought to myself.

I stumbled out of bed, still half asleep and walking like a zombie, and I flipped on the light switch.

The light didn't come on.

I flipped it up and down several more times, but still there was no light. It was then that I noticed the AC was off.

What was going on here?

I pulled back the curtain and saw nothing but pitch black. It was still nighttime. I looked at my phone to check the time (I hadn't brought a watch with me), and it read 4:00 in the morning!

"Oh, this isn't right," I said to myself.

I looked out the window to try and find the satanic creature that was still crowing every minute but could not see him. The windows were rectangular, five feet off the ground, and complete with bars. So, it was hard to see out of them.

I watched cartoons as a kid, and I knew roosters were supposed to crow when the sun rose. This bird was obviously confused or just sadistic. . . or both.

I stumbled back towards my bed and left the covers off because the room, though still cool, was beginning to become warm. As I went back to sleep, I asked the Lord to kill or silence that rooster or help me to ignore it so that I could acquire some more sleep. I was able to sleep with only an occasional waking as my friend was still at it outside.

When the sun finally rose, I heard the noise of people outside my window. I was excited to see Africa in the light, so I sprang out of bed and looked.

There was a lady cooking food over a small open fire in a long, narrow courtyard. She was using special pots to prepare a meal for her family right outside her front door. Then I saw the little rooster running around the courtyard.

"If I can catch that thing later, I will send him to the infernal regions," I thought to myself.

I made my way to freshen up but found Richard was occupying the restroom.

I secured some items from Brother Arnold so I could get clean since I had nothing with me. I stood in the doorway of his room and asked him the question that had been gnawing at me since 4:00 that morning.

"Why don't we have any light or power?"

Even though it was 8:00 am, there was still no electricity.

"The government turned it off," he said simply.

"What do you mean they turned it off?!" I raged.

"The government controls the power plant, and whenever they want, and for whatever reason, they turn it off," he replied as he handed me various items I needed.

"But. . . what hours of the day do they turn it off?"

"Whenever they want," he said.

I stood there dumbfounded.

"Last night, we were on generator power that the mission had. When the fuel ran out, the generator stopped," he explained.

"When will the power come back on?" I asked.

"We don't know. Whenever the government turns it on, I suppose. I'm planning to give the mission more money so they can keep the generator on at night. That way, we don't lose the AC."

I still could not grasp the idea that the government could do this. Later, I discovered that the power plant was not far from where we were staying.

"What in the world was going on in this country?" I thought.

I began to fear that if things kept going the way they were in America. . . well. . . we would have the same problem.

Don't Destroy the Few Luxuries I Have

When Richard was finished with the bathroom, I made my way over. It was a little antiquated but sufficient. The shower was a stall with two perpendicular walls and a shower curtain to wrap around the other two sides. The only problem was that next to the shower was the toilet, and the toilet paper sat on top of the tank. Apparently, Richard had not closed the curtain properly, so all of the toilet paper was soaking wet (I sure hope he never reads this).

It was bad enough that I had no toothpaste, toothbrush, comb, Q Tips, soap, or deodorant, but then to have the toilet paper sabotaged by a Methodist?! I don't think so!

In the immortal words of Bugs Bunny, "Of course you know this means war."

There is nothing more useless than wet toilet paper. Except for maybe a few so called "Christians" I knew back home. I made a mental note to place the toilet paper somewhere else in the future.

It felt good to get cleaned up, so when I was finished, I proceeded to our breakfast area with newfound confidence. As I walked out of the door to the dining hall, I was filled with excitement. I still could not believe that I was in Africa. God was so good to me to let me see His world.

I hurried outside into an open area. In the center, there was a large room. It was a nice dining room, something I would have expected to see in a tropical place. There were plenty of windows and ceiling fans. Our breakfast was hot oatmeal, fresh fruit, bread, bottled water, and a container of hot water for making tea or instant coffee.

I was warned not to drink the water in the country unless it was bottled or boiled because I could get sick. I was very careful the entire time I was there because I did not want to get sick and miss a minute of the trip.

"This is great!" I thought to myself as I looked at breakfast.

How awesome that I was able to eat fresh cut pineapple and mango, and I didn't mind the hot oatmeal either. . . as long as there was sugar (which there was).

I was a very happy man.

This Can't Be Possible

We left our residence to go to town. I still needed to go to the Brussels Airline office in Freetown to make my baggage claim. This experience honestly defies adequate description.

As we proceeded down the mountain, all along the roads were homes. These were not American style homes. They were much smaller, very poor looking, dwellings. And the people, thousands of people, were all walking and selling their wares. Men, women, and children all had something on their heads that they had just bought or were selling.

Everything I had been unable to figure out and understand during the night now made sense in the daylight.

The homes were little stores. They looked like little huts with shelves in them, and the people who lived in them were selling anything they could to make money. The homes were, in many cases, little more than brick structures with old, metal, rusty roofs and old, wooden doors. There were no luxuries to speak of in the homes. The reason they had been walking at night was because home was just a place they slept and had a family meal. They needed to work to make money, so they walked the streets to buy and sell.

As we continued driving, I saw something I had never witnessed before: the garbage dump. This was different than in America because it was where they burned the garbage. I mentioned earlier that the country always smelled like burning wood, but at that moment, the smell had begun to change and not for the better.

The dump was a 48-acre piece of land committed solely to burning the city's garbage. There were spots of fire and plenty of smoke rising out of the earth, but what was disturbing was the people I saw walking through the smoke and fire.

"Why are they in there?" I asked.

"They are looking for food," Solomon answered.

I was devastated.

"Food," I thought. *"What do they expect to find?"*

I wanted to hop out and take a picture. I was told not to though, because there was a chance that they might come after me and take my camera.

One section of the dump was just small mud and brick homes with rusty metal roofs. There were hundreds of these dwellings, and they were literally right next to each other. We made our way into the main part of the city, and I thought that it would surely get better, but it was not to be. The war had left its mark on the dear country. I could see that, before the war, this was a very nice place. But now, there was only the burnt out remains of what once was and what they were trying to repair. There were some nice buildings, and they were working hard to repair this once beautiful city, but it would take time.

The city had a drainage system in sections, and it ran under the sidewalks. The only problem was that in many places the sidewalk was missing, broken in two, or lying in the drainage area. We joked that if a man were drunk and walked on these sidewalks, he could get busted up real bad.

TAKE NOTE SWIATKOWSKI

How my heart broke for the individuals who were so hungry that they had walked through burning fields to find food.

The garbage dump will forever be etched in my mind, and it will remind me of what my Lord said as He pointed to the burning garbage dump outside Jerusalem.

"And if thy hand offends thee, cut it off: it is better for thee to enter into life maimed, than having two hands to go into hell, into the fire that never shall be quenched: Where the worm dieth not, and the fire is not quenched" (Mark 9:43-44).

In the dump, the flies would lay their eggs and the maggots (worm) would begin to crawl and feed on the rotting food, but eventually, the fire would come along and consume them. However, in hell the worm (and the souls of lost sinners) never dies, and the fire does not consume them.

The people who walked in the fire and smoke at the dump looking for food and relief from their hunger were sad. But how sad is it that, in hell, men and women wander the caverns of Hell with no satisfaction.

Jesus warned of this doom for all people if they would not turn to Him for salvation. The story is told through the rich man and Lazarus.

"And it came to pass, that the beggar died, and was carried by the angels into Abraham's bosom: the rich man also died and was buried; And in hell he lifts up his eyes, being in torments, and seeth Abraham afar off, and Lazarus in his bosom. And he cried and said, 'Father Abraham, have mercy on me, and send Lazarus, that he may dip the tip of his finger in water, and cool my tongue; for I am tormented in this flame.' But Abraham said, 'Son, remember that thou in thy lifetime received thy good things, and likewise Lazarus evil things: but now he is comforted, and thou art tormented. And beside all this, between us and you there is a great gulf fixed: so that they which would pass from hence to you cannot; neither can they pass to us, that would come from thence'" (Luke 16:22-26).

When the rich man died, he became a believer. In fact, all the individuals who are in Hell became believers, and they would be the greatest missionaries and evangelists as they long for their families and friends to be saved to avoid the same fate as themselves. The only problem is, they can never tell anyone because they are trapped in Hell.

People often say they will worry about eternity when they enter it, but it will be too late then. Scripture tells us, "For he saith, I have heard thee in a time accepted, and in the day of salvation have I succored thee: behold, now is the accepted time; behold, now is the day of salvation" (II Corinthians 6:2).

Reader, have you trusted Christ as your Saviour? Are you sure you will go to Heaven when you die? The most important decision will be what you do with Christ. How tragic to have heard the Gospel message and then to have rejected it. There is a real Hell, and Christ warned of it often in scripture. One is not consumed and disappears, nor does one fade away but will walk and burn for all eternity. Please turn to Christ now and ask him to save your soul.

It Pays To Lose Your Luggage

The streets of Freetown were crowded. People and cars were everywhere, but the most dangerous of all were the motorbikes. This was a cheap mode of transportation, and they were everywhere.

There was a police presence, but I am not sure what their job description actually entailed. One thing was for sure, their presence was not for road safety. Solomon often told me their favorite saying: "Better to lose the brakes than the horn." This is their saying because all they did was honk their horns at each other. It was very comical to watch. They did drive on the right side of the road; however, there was very little order to it all. Bikes were weaving in and out of traffic as cars were passing each other on the right and left. Pedestrians had to have their wits about them at all times. On several occasions, as we were out and about, our driver would do some of the craziest things. At those moments, I would just slink down in the back seat and hope no fights broke out.

We found the building that housed Brussels Airline, and it was a nice multi-level building. It even had an elevator. To make a long story short, they told me my bag was still in Jersey, and I needed to fill out a form of what my bag looked like along with its contents. They also told me that my bag was supposed to be on the next flight over and that it would arrive on Friday evening.

"Friday?" I asked with a puzzled look.

I was calm on the outside, but inside I was ready to blow.

"But I have very little clothing, and all my stuff is in there."

They then presented me with a check for one hundred dollars and told me to get what I needed. This was a good amount of money in Africa, and I could get more than enough clothes. If I was careful, I could even have money left over.

They were very friendly, went out of their way to help me, and even expressed concern for my state of affair. I also thought that they didn't need to give me money because they had done nothing wrong. It was due to the incompetence on the part of United/Continental Airline that my bag was lost and still in Jersey.

Wal-Mart Please

We went to the bank, cashed the check, and then proceeded to buy some of the things that I needed.

"Is there a store where I can buy some of the remaining items that I need?" I asked.

There wasn't really a response from anyone except for some shared smirks. I later learned that when you made a statement and received no response, you needed to start paying attention.

So, I asked again.

"Where can I get some clothes?"

"Don't worry, Matt. We are going to a place that sells clothes," Solomon assured me.

Brother Arnold went back to the mission while Solomon and our driver took me to do some shopping.

We made our way through the crowded streets, were finally able to park, and then began to walk. The road was dirt. On each side were wooden huts filled with all sorts of clothes. This was very similar to what one might see when going to a large, outdoor flea market in the States. Even on the ground there were large drop cloths with piles of clothes. We began to look.

"Matt, don't buy anything because they will charge you white man's price," Solomon told me.

"White man's price? What is that?" I said laughing.

"You are white. Because of this, they think you have money, so they will charge you a whole bunch more," he explained.

We continued to look as we walked on.

"Hey, white man!" they began to yell as we made our way slowly up the street.

Now, I'm not the brightest bulb in the package, but I knew they were talking to me simply because I was the only white man around. In fact, I felt like a marshmallow in a bag of charcoal. They were yelling and asking me to come and look at their stuff, but I just stuck like glue to Solomon. He asked what I needed, so I gave him my list.

We found some nice shirts, two pairs of pants, sandals for showering in, towels, socks, and a baseball hat that said NASA on it (all the other ones said Obama). Then I purchased some sunglasses.

Throughout my time in Africa, people would yell out to me, "Obama" and wave to me. I thought it was because I was an American, and I would wave back at them. About a week later, I took off my new sunglasses and noticed, for the first time, the word Obama written on the arm of the glasses. My conservative friends back home would have had a field day if they had seen me.

The whole time we were shopping, Solomon and the vendors were yelling at each other in their dialect over the price of each item. Solomon would throw the item down and walk away, they would scream at him, and then they would look at me with puppy dog eyes begging me to buy their stuff. I just mumbled sorry, put my head down, and walked away.

We did well at the market. I think everything put together cost me around $45.00 in American money. Next, we went to a supermarket (of sorts) and purchased other odds and ends like soap, razors, and various toiletries. These items cost me around $20.00.

In the end, I had money left over. The only things I could not purchase or find were a suit coat, a dress shirt, and a tie. I also knew my camera battery would not last till Friday; however, there was no place to buy a camera. Besides, even if there was, I probably could not afford it.

We left the market and began to drive back. The streets were filled with people, and I am referring to the street itself. I asked if we were on an actual road and if we should even be there. But as we honked the horn, the crowd parted and then quickly filled in behind us. I was in the the center of the back seat and wanted to make a video of this experience. However, I noticed people looking at me, and then, Solomon told me that I needed to stop filming because someone might try to steal the camera.

I quickly shut it off and put it away.

Home Economics Class Pays Off

Back at the mission, I went through my new duds. It was then that I noticed one of the pairs of pants I had purchased was too long. Lee had a mini travel sewing kit that he let me borrow to hem my pants. If I had to do it all over again, I would just cut the pant legs with a pair of scissors and leave it at that.

Back in grade school, we had taken wood shop as well as Home Economics classes, and it was there they had taught us how to sew. So, I found matching thread and began to hem my pants. As I finished, I ran out of thread. Of course, all the other colors that were left were quite different and would show. What other option did I have though?! So, I decided to use the closest red thread I could find. I figured it had worked for Rahab in the Bible, why not for me. With my tan Dockers, I had one leg with tan thread and the other with red.

I was assured by the men in our group that I looked good. I am sure my wife would have had a differing opinion. My sewing job would last the entire trip, and in fact, this is the second time my sewing skills have paid off.

Once, at sixth grade camp, they asked for us to do a 20-yard dash, so I signed up. It was a dash of sewing twenty stitches. Needless to say, I blew them all out of the water.

The Sun Setting Over the Atlantic

The day was pretty well spent, and we were hungry. The veterans of the group decide we would go to a nice restaurant. We rode down the mountain and then along the shoreline. The beach and ocean were both beautiful and inviting. I hoped that one day we might be able to go for a swim.

After a long drive, we finally arrived at our restaurant. Now remember, there were quite a few foreigners in the country at the time. Gold, diamonds, minerals, agriculture, fishing, and farming had brought men from around the world. Thus, the place we went to eat catered primarily to European and American tastes.

Inside, there were some locals hanging out and several playing pool. One man I noticed had a shirt that said "New Jersey" on it.

"Hey, are you from Jersey?" I asked excitedly.

"No. I just have the shirt," he said.

"Oh! I'm from Jersey! Could I take a picture with you?"

He nodded, we took a picture together, and we all had a good laugh.

We were seated on an open patio with a roof where we could see the ocean. With our viewpoint, we were able to watch the sun set over the Atlantic.

This phenomenon was different.

I lived in New Jersey, and I had watched the sun rise over the Atlantic many times. I was thankful to my Saviour that I could see the sun set from the other side of the world.

As I watched the yellow, orange, and red colors of the sun descending in the sky, I began to think of home. I knew that on the other side of the ocean was my family. I had missed them the minute I left home, but I had begun to think of them even more which made me miss them very much. I prayed and asked my heavenly Father to watch over them while I was gone. I knew He would take care of them.

TAKE NOTE SWIATKOWSKI

My first full day in Africa, and all of my needs had been met. God was faithful.

"And He said unto His disciples, 'Therefore I say unto you, Take no thought for your life, what ye shall eat; neither for the body, what ye shall put on. The life is more than meat, and the body is more than raiment. Consider the ravens: for they neither sow nor reap; which neither have storehouse nor barn; and God feedeth them: how much more are ye better than the fowls? And which of you with taking thought can add to his stature one cubit? If ye then be not able to do that thing which is least, why take ye thought for the rest? Consider the lilies how they grow: they toil not, they spin not; and yet I say unto you, that Solomon in all his glory was not arrayed like one of these. If then God so clothe the grass, which is to day in the field, and tomorrow is cast into the oven; how much more will he clothe you, O ye of little faith? And seek not ye what ye shall eat, or what ye shall drink, neither be ye of doubtful mind'" (Luke 12:22-29).

These are truths that we constantly have to remind ourselves of. God never forsakes His own. Though the child of God may experience trials and tribulations, the assuring care from our Father in heaven is always there. My needs were met. In fact, I even had Q-Tips. If I needed something, God provided. If I lacked something, I soon learned that it was not as important as I thought it was, and I could survive just fine without it. I was given money, found the right size clothes, watched the sun set over the Atlantic, was with godly men who were my friends, was blessed with a good meal, and had a safe place to rest my head.

Too many individuals worry from day to day, fear the unknown and known, and desire that which they do not have, yet if they would only look, they would realize that very few lack the basic necessities of life: food, clothing, and shelter. If those three things are there, maybe not always in great supply (and yes, sometimes there are hardships), but they are proof that God provides for us.

What should one say about the individuals in Africa I described and how badly they have suffered? What about them? Again, I think we need to look to scripture and see that when one applies biblical principles to their life, God can, and often will, bless. When one chooses to ignore or only give lip service, then one can expect to face these trials on their own.

The one thought that saddened me the most was the thought of my family. I found myself constantly wishing they were with me, but I knew my Father was in America watching them just as sure as He was with me in Africa.

God was so good to His servant.

Chapter Seven

GETTING ADJUSTED

WEDNESDAY

A Day To Visit the Work

I woke up in the morning, and yes that rooster was still going at it. Later on, I would come face-to-face with him, but I did not know that this morning. I looked for a rock to throw, but there were too many people around. So, I decided to leave him alone.

Brother Arnold and I sat and talked while Richard was in the restroom. We always knew if it was him in there because of the bathroom sink. It was supported by and hung from two metal pipes attached the wall. If you bumped the sink, it would fall off the wall. Richard, without fail, would knock it off the wall every morning. He would mumble and grumble as he put the sink back in place, and we would chuckle as we sat there and listened to him day after day.

Once we were ready to begin our day, we parted company with Lee and Richard as we had done the previous day. They would go take care of their ministry, and we would go about ours.

We rode out along the peninsula to visit some of the schools and churches that had been started under the care of Brother Arnold. Our first stops were the David Arnold High School (the principal was Joseph Amara) and the New Testament Baptist Primary School in Wellington (the head teacher being Mrs. Eleanor Massaquoi). These two schools had hundreds of children in attendance. Each student wore a nice school uniform, they were respectful, and they were excited to be educated. But most of all, they were learning about Jesus Christ.

At the high school, Mr. Amara, the principal, had the students gather in the courtyard and sing the school song. They all sang at the top of their voices, and I was moved by their school spirit.

As we drove, the Muslim mosques remained in plain sight. They were everywhere, and they were fighting for control over the minds of these sweet people. In these schools, there are boys and girls who are Muslim; however, they want to know more about Jesus. The schools Brother Arnold planted have helped to provide a unique opportunity for each child to hear the Bible, memorize scriptures in the Bible, and hear God's word preached, all within the walls of the school.

We left Wellington and continued on to Kissi Town in the Tumbo area. A church was built several years earlier in the town as well as a secondary education building known as the Makripodis Baptist School. Its namesake is Mike Makripodis. He was a godly Christian businessman from western Pennsylvania who has been, and still is, very generous. The Lord has blessed him for his faithfulness. The pastor (and principal of the schools) was a kind man by the name of James Spencer-Sesay.

We walked around and looked at the classrooms as well as the young people who were being taught. The rooms were clean, the students were in their uniforms, but they lacked desks and other basic school supplies. In one case, I saw a group of teenagers who sat four people at a two-man desk. Other classrooms were outdoors under large trees with homemade benches, yet they did not shove or complain. No, they sat and listened to their teacher.

There was a man there who was physically handicapped. He had a bicycle he used to get around; however, instead of handlebars there were pedals. In this fashion, he would pedal around on his bike. I was told that he had been a big help in building the church. He would break rocks, put them in the basket on his bike, and then bring them to the church. He was a man who was glad to have a church and did all he could to have a part in building it.

In Williams Town, right by John O Bay, we stopped at a small church where Sieh Sesayohn was the pastor. I walked inside the little building and immediately noticed that there were no chairs or benches.

"What happened to the seats?" I asked.

"We don't have them," Pastor Sieh said. "The people, when they come to church, bring their own."

I was left speechless.

Can you imagine, in the U.S., telling people to bring their own chairs to church? Comfortable seating, heat, and air conditioning is all provided, yet one often has to beg people to come. In Africa, they walk a mile (rain, shine, heat, or extreme heat) carrying their own chair. . . and still they come. It is a different brand of Christianity that they possess compared to what we have in many lazy, slovenly churches in the U.S.

We rode down a winding path further into the jungle and came to a farm. We easily saw the crops they were planting, but what caught my attention was a giant mound of dirt in the middle of the field.

"What in the world is that?" I thought to myself.

So, I asked.

"It is an ant mound," they said.

It stood seven feet tall and was just as big around. . . if not more!

"Are there ants in there?" I asked with a slight tremble.

"Oh yes, millions of ants," they replied.

Now, I'm like the rest of you. I had heard of African killer ants all my life. I didn't know if it was that kind ant mound or not, and I wasn't about to kick it in order to find out. If they were content to leave me alone, I would follow suit.

We walked into a small village and it was abuzz with excitement. We were on the coast, and the men had returned from fishing. It was the sort of fishing where people took a boat out to sea, dropped a net, and the men on shore pulled in the net. Many fish were caught. . . as well as a giant sea turtle. When I arrived, they had already decapitated the poor fella and were beginning to cut him open. I guess they hadn't gotten the memo that these babies are endangered. These people needed food, and they were all happy.

When I asked if they were going to eat it, they smiled and gave a very emphatic yes. They pointed to a large turtle shell hanging on the outside wall of a hut. So, they had done this before. They asked if I could stay for supper, but I kindly turned down the invitation. They proceeded to go back to work on the big boy, and I snapped some pictures of the whole ordeal. I figured some "save the turtle" person might get a kick out of seeing this.

I looked at my camera and noticed the battery was dying. I normally kept the spare battery in the carrying case. I zipped the small bag open to get it. I figured it would have plenty of life to hold me over until Friday when my luggage arrived. But my heart sank when it wasn't there.

"What happened to it?" I thought.

Little did I know in that moment, nor would I find out until I returned home, that my dear wife had told me she had taken it out before I left and put it on the charger. I was supposed to put it all in the suitcase before I left. Obviously, that didn't happen.

A sense of frustration began to sweep over me, and I started to get mad. I wanted to take as many pictures as I possibly could! I did not want to miss recording one aspect of this adventure! Now, to be here and have no camera, well. . . Satan was using that to stir me up and become angry. I had to let it go. This had been such a great day so far, and I knew it would get better. So, I chose to trust the Lord and see what would happen.

We proceeded down a winding dirt road that was very steep. It led to the ocean, and I had never seen or experienced anything like what I saw.

Gilligan's Island Can't Touch This

At the bottom of the road were some grass huts. There were no walls. Just some poles holding up a grass roof. But beyond the huts, there was the prettiest lagoon I had ever laid eyes on. With the lagoon on one side, a very long sandy reef and the ocean on the other side of the reef, well, it was a sight to behold.

As I walked out onto the beach, I looked over to the lagoon. There was a man in a long wooden boat, the kind of boat carved from a tree. He was holding a long pole. I looked over to the left where the ocean met the beach. In the whitest sand, every hundred yards or so, were large black rocks cropping up where the waves would crash around.

"Matt, we are going to go swimming!" Brother Arnold said with a smile.

"But, we didn't bring anything to swim in," I interjected.

Right about then a father and son came walking down the beach pretty much the same way Adam looked when God first made him. I thought *"he doesn't mean that we will go swimming like that?!"* But before I could say anything else, Brother Arnold reassured me.

"The pastor just went to grab us some suits. Don't worry."

Now, I had been taking notes and according to my research, there were not too many people built like me in this country. Everyone I had encountered so far were all lean and muscular, and I was. . . well. . . a little stockier. Let's put it this way, if I were a kid, I would be in the husky section. But I shouldn't have worried, because he quickly came back with two suits.

On the lagoon side were some grass huts, and I quickly ran in one to change. No doors, but there were three walls and a roof. The bathing suit fit! Isn't God good? I ran to the water as fast as I could. The lagoon was perfect as I swam around and cooled off. I laid on my back in the water and looked at the shore. Tree covered mountains, grass huts, white sand, beautiful palm trees, and crystal-clear water.

"This is truly a paradise," I thought.

It couldn't get prettier than this. If one didn't know any better, it looked like a place that had never been touched by war.

The man in the boat said he would give me a ride around the lagoon . . . for a price. I needed to be careful with my money, so I kindly told him no. I walked onto the sandy reef and then jumped into the ocean. I had never swam in water like this. I had travelled up and down the East Coast of the States and even the Bahamas, but this beach was beyond compare.

We swam and talked for about an hour until the natives began to yell for us to come in. Brother Arnold told me it was for lunch.

"Lunch," I thought to myself. *"What lunch?"*

The men who lived here had caught lobster and fish for us, and they had cooked it on an open fire. They had also prepared some brown rice. I thought I had died and gone to heaven. This beach, the food, and the people were outstanding, and I could not believe that my God had allowed me to experience it all. Why should I say such things? My Father loves me and is very gracious.

We ate our meal, and unfortunately, we had to go. It was at this exact point in my trip that my camera finally died. What was I to do? I was in Africa, and I had no camera. Although it was true that my phone had a camera, it was dying as well.

"Father, why would you let me go to Africa and not let me have a camera?" I asked silently.

But just as he had up to this point, God would continue to provide for me.

TAKE NOTE SWIATKOWSKI

"Thou wilt keep him in perfect peace, whose mind is stayed on thee: because he trusteth in thee" (Isaiah 26:3).

How easy it is for us to forget all the good things God has done for us at the first moment of trouble. I had let my eyes wonder off of God's goodness and care and had allowed something so foolish as a camera to aggravate me. Looking back on this trip, I have over two thousand pictures of Africa (from this trip up to when I would return the next year). Had I honestly believed that the Lord did not know the desire of my heart? Sure He did, and He was gracious to a grown man who was acting very childish in his heart.

Yet, how many Christians do the same thing over so many different desires, obstacles, and longings in life?

When I was in Bible College, I had a friend who was mad at God. He told me that he was giving God two weeks to give him a girlfriend, and if God didn't, he was leaving the school. Here was a young man studying to be a preacher and acting so spiritually immature.

I told him that he just needed to be patient. He needed to know that our Father would meet his need in His time, and I jokingly told him that he wasn't that good looking so the Lord was having to work on some dear girl's heart right then. He laughed and agreed to give God some more time

It's sad knowing that Christianity is filled with this attitude of not trusting God and not believing that He does all things well. Far too many people quit attending church and walk away from God because they believe He didn't treat them right or fairly. But let's be honest, it's them who didn't treat the Lord right, and they know it in their heart.

While they were unsaved, they lived in sin and rebellion against the Lord and His righteous standard. Now that they are saved, they act like the Lord should be doing cartwheels for them. Salvation and God doesn't work that way.

Once, a man I had known approached me and told me that he had stabbed his Bible, cursed God out, and walked away from the faith. When I asked him why he did this, he told me it was because he didn't have a wife. I was very open and honest with him. I reminded him of how he had been living in fornication (and even adultery) with women, and God would not bless that sin. He became very angry and defensive when I said this and told me that God was obligated to bless him because He said so in the Bible. Again, I told him he was misinformed and ignorant of scripture. We talked for some time, but he refused to acknowledge his sin and continued to curse God.

Christians, God is good all the time, He is Holy all the time, and what He does is always right. Believe that and rest in it. This truth will keep you in perfect peace.

The Sadder Side Of Life

After our swim and lunch at the lagoon, we made our way back to Freetown. It was not that far of a ride, but the traffic made it take hours. When we finally arrived back at the mission, we cleaned up.

The next day was to be a preacher's conference, and pastors from all over would be coming to Freetown to be part of the event. It would be in the evening, and Pastor Joseph Mosseray would be there.

We all wanted something to eat as the lobster and fish had worn off. Brother Arnold recommended getting something from the Family Kingdom. Solomon stayed back with Brother Arnold so they could discuss some business. Pastor Joseph, the driver, and I would go grab the food.

The Family Kingdom was a large hotel that sat on Lumley Beach. It was night time when I saw it for the first time. There was a large wall that encircled and surrounded three sides of the hotel, and at the front, there was a gate to enter by. On both sides, at the front of the building, were two restaurants. . . both within the wall and gates. I could not understand why there were walls and gates, but again, there is a reason for everything.

We placed our order at one of the restaurants, just hamburgers and fries. The Family Kingdom was owned by a Lebanese family, and its sole source of guests were foreigners. It was a very nice place with rooms of every size and shape. Some of the buildings were four stories tall, others were just two. There were also some bungalow style rooms available. Later on the trip,

I would stay here and find the rooms very clean. They also had their own source of electricity that was never turned off.

As we sat on the patio waiting, we talked and made pleasant conversation, but I noticed something going on out on the street. The Family Kingdom hotel stood on one side of the main road and the beach and ocean were directly on the other side of the street. The hotel, which was a place for out-of-towners (or shall I say, rich foreigners), attracted what one might refer to as "the women of the night." They walked up and down the street dressed in the best possible clothing they could find, but I could not help but feel so sorry for them. During the day, there was no sign of them.

I began to grow angry at the men who took advantage of such desperate people. As we sat there, they called out to us and said things that I could not really understand, but I did not need to understand the words. I knew what they wanted.

The wait for food was long, and many a man was seen taking a young lady through the gates and into the hotel. There was a serious AIDS epidemic in Africa, so for a man to solicit one of these young ladies was a dangerous thing. In fact, there were billboards all across the country warning of the dangers of AIDS and how it's spread. And on this note, I have a heartbreaking story to share later on.

TAKE NOTE SWIATKOWSKI

While watching the street in front of the hotel, I was reminded of what God said about this lifestyle.

"For at the window of my house I looked through my casement, And beheld among the simple ones, I discerned among the youths, a young man void of understanding, Passing through the street near her corner; and he went the way to her house, In the twilight, in the evening, in the black and dark night: And, behold, there met him a woman with the attire of a harlot, and subtle of heart. (She is loud and stubborn; her feet abide not in her house:

Now is she without, now in the streets, and lieth in wait at every corner.) So she caught him, and kissed him, and with an impudent face said unto him, "I have peace offerings with me; this day have I payed my vows. Therefore came I forth to meet thee, diligently to seek thy face, and I have found thee. I have decked my bed with coverings of tapestry, with carved works, with fine linen of Egypt. I have perfumed my bed with myrrh, aloes, and cinnamon. Come, let us take our fill of love until the morning: let us solace ourselves with loves. For the good man is not at home, he is gone a long journey: He hath taken a bag of money with him and will come home at the day appointed." With her much fair speech she caused him to yield, with the flattering of her lips she forced him. He goeth after her straightway, as an ox goeth to the slaughter, or as a fool to the correction of the stocks; Till a dart strike through his liver; as a bird hasteth to the snare, and knoweth not that it is for his life. Hearken unto me now therefore, O ye children, and attend to the words of my mouth. Let not thine heart decline to her ways, go not astray in her paths. For she hath cast down many wounded: yea, many strong men have been slain by her. Her house is the way to hell, going down to the chambers of death" (Proverbs 7:6-27).

What King Solomon described could be seen that night on the streets of Freetown. Men and women do not change, and truth does not change. Men and women alike were destroying their lives. One was doing it for money while the other was doing it for a few moments of pleasure, but in the end, death will be the result.

"For the lips of a strange woman drop as honeycomb, and her mouth is smoother than oil: But her end is bitter as wormwood, sharp as a two-edged sword. Her feet go down to death; her steps take hold on hell" (Proverbs 5:3-5).

Cheeseburger, Cheeseburger, Cheeseburger

We received our order and proceeded back to the room. I was hungry, and a delicious hamburger sounded really good. A person hasn't lived 'till they have bitten into a hamburger, had some grease drip down their arm, had the remnants of ketchup on the side of their mouth, and had some of the burger blow out on the opposite side of where you were biting. But this burger was a little different. I believe it was beef, but I didn't ask for conscience sake. It had coleslaw, ketchup, mustard, and mayo on it. You may think that doesn't sound bad, but there was something different about this coleslaw.

I don't know what it was, but it was different.

It was good, and it kept me alive. . . but it was different.

The french fries, on the other hand, were very good! I don't care where you are in the world, you have to eat french fries where you order them. Once you put them into a bag and take them on a journey, they morph into something else entirely.

We all ate and talked but knew it was time for bed.

This was a good day.

I was encouraged by seeing all the churches and the schools. God was working in Africa, and people's lives were being changed by the Gospel of my Saviour, Jesus Christ.

Chapter Eight

SOLDIER STREET

THURSDAY

Pictures Please

"Matt, would you mind taking pictures and videos of the meeting today?" Brother Arnold asked me that morning.

"I'd love to, but I can't. My camera battery died yesterday, and I don't have a charger with me," I sadly replied .

"Well God love ya! Here, use my camera," he said as he passed his camera over to me.

"You have a camera?" I asked completely dumfounded.

"Yes, of course! Do you think you could use it today?"

"I think I can manage," I replied.

When he showed me his camera, my hopes sunk just a bit. It was definitely a camera but a little outdated. However, it was better than mine since mine wasn't even working.

Brother Arnold's camera was actually a video camera that still used a small tape to record video, but it had a camera feature as well that used an SD card. There was no flash. . . just a light you could turn on when making a video. I knew all my inside shots would be dark. I would need as much light as possible to get them to be clear. But even so, this was an answer to prayer. I had prayed the day before about a camera, and little did I know, the Lord had one the entire time! God had brought me to Africa, and He had given me a camera as well. I made sure it was all charged up, and we proceeded to our meeting.

Meeting the Men and Woman Behind the Scenes

Ever since I first met Brother Arnold, he talked about Soldier Street Baptist Church, and today, I saw it for the first time. It was somewhat surreal to be there in-person.

A conference was held at the church in honor of Bishop Max Gorvie who was retiring as overseer of the work in Sierra Leone. Over 42 preachers were present. There were old and young preachers alike. School teachers and principals from the schools were also in attendance. These dear people had traveled many miles, and they were excited about what God was doing. The pastor of the church, during that time, was Joseph Mosseray. All of the preachers and teachers who I had met the day before were there, so I didn't feel like such a stranger.

The church building had been touched by the war, and the marks were evident. When the rebels were in the capital a few years earlier, they came down Soldier Street. Young Theophilus Gorvie stood at the top of the stairs and told the rebels they could not enter the church because it was God's house. They took their guns, struck him to the ground, and made their way into the church. But the young man would not be stopped. Bleeding and hurting, he made his way to the front of the church and told them again to leave God's house. The rebels were wicked men. They had killed, raped, and maimed untold thousands. Unspeakable crimes had been committed by them, and as many were on drugs and demon possessed, they had little value for human life. They stared at this young man for a little while, took their guns, and began to spray the walls with bullets. . . but only the side and the back. They left Theophilus alone, as well as the front of the church. When they had finished, they turned around and left.

When I looked around, I saw how horrible war was and the devastation that it had left behind. The neighborhood where the church stood was a sad sight. Most countries rebuild and try to move on, but this country was struggling to do that. There were reconstruction projects going on, but it was evident it would take years.

The purpose of the meeting involved Max Gorvie. He would be stepping down as the overseer of the churches and schools. He had spent many years establishing and then visiting them the same way the Apostle Paul had. He was just as concerned about the churches he had established as Paul was. It was in this meeting that Solomon would take his father's place.

Now, just so we're clear, these were independent churches; however, because the country is so poor, the average pastor and school would not survive without outside help. The churches are supported by World Evangelistic Outreach and Solomon was there to make sure there was accountability.

Be Kind to Strangers, They Will Clear Traffic

It was lunchtime, so Brother Arnold and I went into town to get a bite to eat. The people from the meeting were eating lunch at the church. We wanted to join them, but there was a good chance that the food they prepared might not be good for us. There was the possibility that it might have contained some bacteria that would make us sick. Solomon was always careful to make sure we did not eat anything that would make a white man sick. The Africans were used to the food and microscopic creatures, but we, on the other hand, were not. Because of this fact, it could cause us serious harm.

The place we went for lunch was somewhere Brother Arnold loved to go. It was called Crown Bakery, and it catered to foreigners. Brother Arnold liked to say he was going to C.B. and that it stood for Christian Businessmen Association. Outside the restaurant were groups of homeless men who begged for food and money. All of them knew Brother Arnold.

"Hey preacher!" they began to yell when they saw him.

He talked to all of them. He promised to get them a large sack of rice later, and sure enough, he would. They were all kind souls. One could not help but feel for them and begin to love them.

Once inside the bakery, I was taken aback by all the fair skinned people I saw. Most, if not all, were Europeans. I enjoyed listening to all of the languages that were spoken, but I also wondered what brought them to Freetown. What type of business were they in? We were here on business for the King of Kings and nobody had a greater or worthier job than us.

We finished lunch and made our way to the car. Again, the men came running to Brother Arnold. He gave them all a few dollars, and they were happy. The streets were crowded, and one man in particular took a real liking to us.

This dear man had some sort of mental illness which caused us not to be able to understand a word he said. He began to yell and wave his arms. I was not sure what was going to happen next, but it was a real treat. He got in front of our car and began to run in front of us, yelling and clearing traffic. Even the police got out of his way! Cars pulled over and people jumped back. He ran for a good mile doing this the entire time. Pedestrians were looking to see who was screaming, and believe me, he was yelling. If I had seen him coming at me, I would have gotten out of the way, too. The whole time, we were crying with hysterics of laughter as he cleared traffic for us. Oh, where was my camera when I needed it? When he stopped, Brother Arnold gave him some more money, and he was happy as could be.

We never did see him again, but I will never forget him.

Back to the Meeting

When we returned to the church, it was my turn to preach.

I was a little intimidated.

I apologized for my clothing because if there was one thing an African liked it was for an American to dress like an American. By this I mean a suit and tie when it came time for church. They were all dressed in their Sunday best, and I stood there in a polo, Dockers, and deck shoes. They all laughed when I explained my clothing dilemma, and I believe they all felt bad for me.

I looked out at the people, many of which had survived war, many had lost family members and had seen and experienced cruelty beyond description.

What could I say to help them?

I learned, many years ago, that even when I think I have nothing to offer, God does. He has a book we call the Bible, and when preached in His power, it changes lives. So, I stood and preached about Jesus and His word. When I finished, they all came up to me, shook my hand, hugged my neck, and told me thank you. Then, a few of them (in the Krio language) pointed at my clothes and laughed. . . all in good fun of course.

TAKE NOTE SWIATKOWSKI

"And ye became followers of us, and of the Lord, having received the word in much affliction, with joy of the Holy Ghost" (I Thessalonians 1:6).

"Therefore, brethren, we were comforted over you in all our affliction and distress by your faith" (I Thessalonians 3:7).

The church Paul wrote to was a group of believers that had suffered great affliction. They had suffered simply because they were Christians. The Apostle wrote to encourage them. He was encouraged in return by the faithfulness and joy they portrayed even through their trials.

When I sat in church the day of the meeting, I saw people who had lived through terrible atrocities. Many of them had personally experienced the suffering. I learned that the rebels were still among the people, and after the war, they blended back into society. How do you react when you see a man who murdered a family member, raped your wife or daughter, or cut off your arm or leg? This is what they lived with in Africa, and yet, they were still in church singing and eager to hear from God. I was moved and encouraged by them. I needed to hear from them, I needed to have their type of Christianity. They were a testimony of the grace of God.

Eat Your Supper! There Are People Starving In Africa.

When we left, we proceeded to the home of Max Gorvie. It sat on the side of a hill in Freetown near the Congo River. It was a nice little home, and Brother Max lived there with his children and family. As I stood outside of the house on the patio, I saw a young man running up a long staircase cut into the hill. In his hand, he was carrying something that I could not quite make out. When he got closer, it became obvious what he held. It was a very large, dead rat. He was holding it by the tail.

"What do you have there?" I yelled over to him.

With a large smile, he held it high to show me.

"Did you kill that?" I asked.

He smiled even wider and nodded yes.

"How?" I probed.

He picked up a rock and threw it to the ground.

I understood what he meant. He simply stoned it to death.

"What are you going to do with it? Eat it?"

"Yes!" He said, still smiling.

He posed for a few snap shots and then continued running up the stairs thoroughly excited about his meal for the evening.

This scene put a whole new perspective on the suffering the people of Sierra Leone faced. These people were so hungry that they saw a rat as a great meal.

From there, we proceeded back to our rooms, cleaned up, and had a nice supper of chicken, rice, and a salad. All I could think about was that poor man and his supper.

I was doing well. I was being fed. But that boy had to fight every day of his life to secure a meal and stay alive.

Some Have Compassion and Make a Difference

When we finished eating, Brother Arnold wanted some ice cream. We drove down to the Family Kingdom and sat in one of the restaurants in front of the hotel. We sat there with iron bars between us and the street. We walked out of the restaurant after eating our ice cream headed for the car. As we did, three young ladies from the street approached us. They came with all of the usual dialogue and were doing their best to be seductive. With Solomon, Brother Arnold, and myself standing there, I stated that we were preachers, as well as married men, and we were not interested. When this was said, the countenance of all three changed completely. They went from being bold and seductive to what they really felt: scared and frightened. They began to tear up and asked if we would pray for them. They were poor, sick, and some even had children at home who needed food. That's why they were working the streets. While we were talking, I could tell they felt ashamed by the way they had their heads hung low. It was really a very pitiful sight, and my heart went out to them.

They claimed to be Christians and said they had been saved. Now, I know some may say that if they were really saved, they wouldn't do what they did for a living. All I will say to that is this: we should always be careful what we think. We prayed with those young girls, and they walked off into the darkness. My heart broke, and again, I grew angry at the men who would be so cruel to use these girls in such a way.

TAKE NOTE SWIATKOWSKI

"Ye are of your father the devil, and the lusts of your father ye will do. He was a murderer from the beginning, and abode not in the truth, because there is no truth in him. When he speaketh a lie, he speaketh of his own: for he is a liar, and the father of it" (John 8:44).

Jesus told us that Satan was a murderer, and that is just what he is. Everything he promises is a lie, and it will lead to death.

The prodigal ran off. He left his home and family in order to look for the good life, he did not realize that he was leaving the best behind. I am certain Satan spoke to his heart and told him how mean his father was, how hard the work was, and that if he could just get out on his own, then he would have freedom and liberty and could begin to enjoy life.

The best life one will ever have is in the will of God. It may not be glamorous, it may not be fun, but it will be safe and bring true joy. As a pastor, I have seen many a person run off into sin and not too many have come back. The ones that did return had the scars to show for all their, so called, "fun."

There are no regrets or scars in the service of Jesus Christ.

I often think of my time in Africa. Many of the young girls who walked that street at night are now in eternity. Disease had caught up to them, and the joy Satan promised was just a lie. He ended up murdering them. How many men who couldn't control their lust, who lived to feed their flesh, also contracted some disease and died? And if they lived, how many lived with pain and suffering for just a few moments of sinful pleasure?

Chapter Nine

OFF INTO THE PROVINCES

FRIDAY

The Needs Are Met

My luggage was supposed to arrive on Friday, but we received word that the plane would not land until that evening. The airline would not bring my bags to our lodgings until Saturday morning. So, I had to wait one more day for my things. To be quite honest though; I did not lack anything. It's true I couldn't use my own camera, but God gave me one to use. The cell phone I had was dying, but when I looked at Brother Arnold's, I noticed that his charger would work on my phone as well. My phone was charged, but it still wouldn't dial out, so I could not call home. However, Brother Arnold let me use his to call whenever I wanted.

Today was a slow day as Solomon was busy in town getting all the necessary paperwork for our trip into Liberia next week. This took much longer than we anticipated. While he was out, we went down to Lumley beach. While we were there, we could eat at the restaurant. As I said before, there were only two restaurants: one on each side of the hotel entrance. We bought our hamburgers from the restaurant to the right of the hotel, and then, we went over to the restaurant on the left.

This restaurant was owned by a husband and wife, and they had some small children. They also were Lebanese and were very nice. The dear lady had a sad countenance about her. I wondered why she looked so sad. She was a young lady, quite pretty, and her husband seemed to treat her well.

One never knows what's going on in a person's life. So often, many people hide their pain or suffering, but there are others who cannot hide it and it shows on their face.

I felt bad for the woman at the restaurant. Every time I saw her, she had this look about her. Maybe she was fine, and it was her normal look. Then again, maybe it wasn't. We talked with them, and they told us they were Lebanese Christians, and someday, they hoped to have a place of their own where they wouldn't have to pay rent to the Family Kingdom.

After talking with them, we walked up and down the beautiful beach. We watched the fishermen bring their nets in and had an enjoyable and relaxing day. My first thought was that we should have been busy doing something, but the Lord gave us the day to relax because He knew that the next week would be a different story.

Learning to Deal With It

Saturday morning came. We said goodbye to the mission, enjoyed our last breakfast there, and then said goodbye to Lee and Richard. They were going out into the country but in a different location from us. We would see them again next week and travel home with them. In the meantime, it was time to pick up my luggage at the Brussels airline office.

When we walked into the office, I saw a pile of suitcases. My heart jumped as I thought I saw mine, but much to my dismay, it wasn't there. I kept grabbing ones I thought might be mine, but it always ended up as someone else's. The people in the office were genuinely concerned for me and looked disappointed. . . but not as disappointed as I was.

"Where is my luggage?" I asked.

I was a little irritated. I didn't want it to show because they knew I was a preacher, and I did not want to ruin my testimony.

"We don't know where it is. At the last check, it was in Brussels. We will put a search on for it right away," they told me.

Walking out of the office, I was angry. I had it in my head that somewhere along the line someone had stolen it, and I verbally expressed this concern to Solomon.

"Who would steal your suitcase?" Solomon asked as he laughed.

I looked at him and had no answer because even I knew it was a dumb thought.

"I don't know, but someone has my luggage," I said as I shrugged my shoulders.

It's times like these that you have to stop, look, and realize your needs have been met. I had clothes, toiletries, and a camera. Even so, it was the fact that my stuff was missing that was irritating me. I had gifts in there to give out, and I could no longer do that. My sermons were in my bag. . . as well as handouts for the meetings.

But just as He always did, God provided and took care of me. My anger was nothing but selfishness and pride. God was working on me through the situation, though I couldn't see it at that point, and I eventually realized that I would ruin my trip if I let the anger brew inside of me.

Over the years, I have watched people throw away some good times and good people in their lives over small and insignificant things.

TAKE NOTE SWIATKOWSKI

"Take us the foxes, the little foxes, that spoil the vines: for our vines have tender grapes" (Song of Solomon 2:15).

God, in his wisdom, reveals truth to us, and one of those truths is that it's the little things that spoil us.

I had to face the fact that I would have to live without my stuff, and thinking about it and growing angry would not help me. I would like to say that this was the end of it; however, flare ups continued throughout the week, and I had to deal with them as they arose.

I had the time of my life seeing a new country and making new friends. My heart was encouraged by the people and the preaching. I loved the car rides and all the villages. I enjoyed the food and Fanta orange soda (even the apple soda was delicious). Everything was great. Yet, the thought of my suitcase spoiled my time, and I sat and fumed over this.

How foolish I was!

I have seen many preachers do this all the time. They can have a full church, see people saved, and yet, they will go home trying to figure out who wasn't in church and choose to stew on that instead of the blessings God gave.

I have seen many Christians do this when they have so much, yet they choose to concentrate on what they don't have and let it make them become bitter.

Certainly, scripture is true when it says that the little things ruin us.

SATURDAY

Leaving As Good As It's Going to Get

We said goodbye to Freetown and made our way into the provinces. I did not understand this term of "provinces" when I first heard it but was afraid to ask what they meant. To put it simply, it was the area of the country made up of little villages. Hotels, restaurants, and paved roads were behind us.

"I'm leaving behind the best it's going to be. It's going to get worse from here on out," I thought to myself as we were preparing to leave.

I'll be honest, I was having trouble adjusting to Africa. I did not tell this to anybody. I had too much pride to admit it, and besides, I was still having a good time. However, I was spoiled as an American. I did not want to complain to Brother Arnold or tell him that I was worried about what might be out in the provinces. He had enough on his plate and did not need me whining and complaining. Too often, people become self-centered, complain, and fail to realize they are being annoying.

We hopped into our Toyota 4Runner and made our way out of town. Our vehicle was comfortable, but the tires were a sight to behold. When I first saw them, I thought, *"We are not going to make it!"*

I had heard of missionaries dying as their tires blew out on some old, dirt road, and I thought to myself, *"Well Lord, I may be coming home soon."*

We drove for three hours on paved roads but could not exceed 45 mph because of the tires. I looked out of the window and tried to soak in all that I saw. National Geographic wasn't lying when they showed the pictures of the natives. It was all there: huts, men, and women carrying things on their heads. There it was, and I was taking it in. I was having a good time.

As we were driving, the paved road ended turning into dirt suddenly. I wondered when the paved road would begin again, but it was a foolish thought. I discovered it was all hard, clay roads from now on.

It was hot.

I was sitting in the back seat when I fell asleep. I don't know how long I was out, but I was woken up suddenly by a very loud bang.

We blew the rear tire.

Here we were, in the middle of nowhere, with no spare and the nearest village a few miles back. Our driver jacked up the car and removed the tire. Then Solomon took out a knife and began to cut the tire away. He did this because the tire was beyond any repair.

"It will take forever to cut that tire off," I told him.

"You know Matt, they have a proverb here in Africa, 'the longest of journeys begins with a single step,'" He calmly said.

I thought to myself, *"That's a Chinese proverb,"* but I kept silent.

When I looked up from Solomon, I saw a lone figure coming down the road. As he came closer, he looked even stranger. His hair was greatly disheveled, and he was dirty as if he had not bathed in a very long time. His pants were ragged; he wore a leather shoulder bag, a dirty long sleeve shirt, and a wool hat. I asked the guys who he was, and they said he was a bushman. I never asked anymore and just took that to mean he lived in the jungle and ate off the land. He came closer and helped with the changing of the tire.

Our driver, Marcel, took the rim and ran to the next village to get it fixed. I may have been sleeping, but I sure didn't remember there being a Michelin dealer anywhere. We sat around and talked while we waited. People walked by on the road, and we said hello. After an hour or so, Marcel came back rolling a new tire with him. He put it on, and we headed up the road.

We arrived at our destination. It was in the town of Moriba, and we were staying at a mining camp. It was a British owned mining company who employed men from all around the world. They mined for Rutile. Rutile is a mineral (Titanium Dioxide) that has many uses; however, its primarily used as a whitener in paints, paper, and textile.

The camp was on a hill. They had a security gate, and we had to provide proper ID each time we entered. There were many cabins in the camp, very similar to trailers you find in the South of the United States. The camp had also faced the ravages of the war, and many houses were burnt to the ground with just the concrete pad and some twisted metal left. There were office buildings, tennis courts, a big inground swimming pool, and a large dining room. We ate our meals in the dining room, and the food was pretty good. You have to remember that this was where they served all the workers, so they had to provide good meals.

These men would work for about three months, go home for a few weeks, and then come back again. This was a difficult life for a married man. The miners would spend their off hours downtown because of the bars and other places they could indulge their sinful desires.

Where we were staying was only the camp, the actual mining areas were out in the countryside. You could tell where they had been mining because of a large greenish blue lake that was left behind. Water is used in the extraction of the mineral, and the lake is clean and harmless.

We went to our cabin after our meal, talked for several hours, and then retired to our rooms. They were clean and comfortable. Everyday a cleaning lady would come in, make up the beds, and do our laundry. Later on, she would come back carrying the laundry basket on her head with the clothes folded nice and neat inside. I still marvel at how she was able to balance the basket on her head while walking.

SUNDAY

The Lords Day and Church Dedication

I woke up early Sunday morning. In fact, it was 3:00 am when I looked at the clock. As I walked out of my room, I saw Brother Max Gorvie praying and reading his Bible.

"It's no wonder this man has started 26 churches and 12 schools. He certainly is a man of God," I thought to myself.

I was humbled being there with him.

We ate breakfast and then made our way into the village. When we reached the church, the building was crowded, and everyone was in their Sunday best. The church was new. It was a long cement block building with several large openings on the sides for windows. The doors were not yet installed. Inside the room, there were wooden benches for the congregation to sit on. Not only did this building serve as the church sanctuary, but it was also being used as a Christian schoolhouse. I could feel the excitement buzzing around me.

I soon discovered that the one thing everyone was most excited about was the new bathroom that was being installed. So, we went outside to take a look.

At that moment, there was only a large hole in the ground. The hole was rectangular in shape and well over ten feet deep. Next year, they would have the rest of the bathroom built. Boy's and girl's rooms would be installed. We would call this "bathroom" pit toilets or a large outhouse. But they were excited, and I guess it would be better than the alternative of finding a spot in the jungle. Later, (on a future trip) I asked where one of the preachers had gone. They sheepishly told me he had gone into the woods and was covering his feet. It took me a minute to get it, I but figured it out. After all, I have read the Bible.

I was able to preach to everyone that morning with an interpreter. If you have never preached this way, you may find it extremely frustrating as I did. It was easy to almost lose my train of thought while the interpreter was talking over me. It was here that I learned how much I needed the Lord.

So often, preachers think that because of their smooth, flowing words and voice fluctuations that God is working. But this thought is so sad because it is never us at all. As a child of God, we need the Holy Spirit to do the work in people's hearts. We have very little to do with it.

After the service, we hung around and talked to the people, took photographs, and then headed back to the mining camp for lunch and a meeting.

There were a few moments of free time that day, and I began to walk around the camp to see the sights. As I was walking, I heard some noises coming from the jungle. I was told that there was no wildlife in Sierra Leone. This was because during the war, rebels shot anything that moved.

I listened.

I was straining my eyes, squinting into the jungle, to see what the noise was and where it had come from.

Then I heard it again.

Above me, I saw monkeys swinging in the trees. I tried to snap a picture with the camera I had, but unfortunately, the zoom had its limitations.

I was beyond excited to see monkeys in the wild. There they were, having the time of their lives swinging at the top of the trees as if it took no effort. I was so happy and grateful to my Heavenly Father that He had allowed me to see that incredible sight.

That afternoon, we headed to the village of Gbanbama (Bang bama). Brother Max Gorvie was with us as he was the overseer of the church and schools. We had driven out to the village to dedicate their new church building to the Lord. The place was crowded with people, and all of them seemed to know Brother Arnold. We all met in the middle of the village where there was a large marching band (complete with all the brass instruments, percussions, cymbals, and even the blue and white band outfits).

They placed Brother Arnold on a large hammock that was supported by poles on each side. The men had planned to carry him around with the band out front and the people marching and singing behind him as they made their way to the new church. No sooner had Brother Arnold gotten into the hammock then he rolled out of it and onto the ground.

There was a collective gasp.

Men and women began yelling, and people started running to help him up. He was on the ground rolling over (trying to get up) his pride completely crushed. And there I stood, holding the camera, trying to stop myself from laughing hysterically as tears rolled down my cheeks, all the while trying to take pictures. Brother Arnold was dusted off, placed back in the hammock, and the parade resumed.

It was a sight to behold.

We made our way to the church. When we reached the threshold, we stopped and had a prayer of dedication at the front door. The village chief, who was an elderly lady, ran that village with an iron fist. . . even the men were afraid of her, and so was I. She was very sweet, but no one wanted to cross her. She was addressed as the Paramount Chief and called Madam Hawa. Her full name was Hawa Kpanabom Sokaw. She had been the chief since 1983. Each village had a chief, and if anything was to be done, it had to be cleared by the chief. This dear lady had come to know Christ. She was saved and converted from the Muslim faith, and she was excited to see a church that was built and going to be used for the glory of her God and Saviour.

Everyone filed into the building for the service to begin. The service went on for several hours with congregational singing, special songs, scripture readings, and sermons.

It was very hot in the church (and I mean hot), and being the very spiritual man that I am, I found myself wishing I was in the swimming pool back at the mining camp. The new building did not come with air conditioning . . . not even ceiling fans. It was the kind of hot that made you fall asleep. So, there I was, sitting in a prominent place, trying not to fall asleep.

Oh, how I hated it!

Every now and then a child would get loud and start to fool around with a friend. It was nothing out of the ordinary for mom to reach over and wallop him, and I mean wallop! The children were taught not to cry out, or it would get worse. Nobody flinched. No police were called, no threats against the family were made. All that happened was the child would sit quietly and gently rub whatever part of the body that was hurting. They learned to respect their parents and the church service. When this sort of discipline happened, and it happened in several places and times on the trip, I would put my head down and start to chuckle thinking of what would happen back in the U.S. if someone disciplined their child in the middle of a service in this manner.

Brother Arnold and the villagers all wanted photographs taken. Although the camera worked well outdoors, it would be a dark picture indoors because the old camera had no flash and there was no electricity in the church building.

Afterwards, there was a dinner held on the grounds. Everyone ate and had a great time. I tried my best to talk to everyone while enjoying myself. I noticed that several people from the village we were at that morning were in attendance, and I asked how they got there.

"They all walked," explained Brother Arnold.

"How far away is it?" I asked.

"Well . . ." he paused in thought. "It would take them about seven hours to get here."

Oh my soul!

In Africa, these people had walked seven hours to go to a church service, while in America, there were so many who wouldn't even walk a block or drive twenty minutes to go to church. What dear, godly, and faithful people. They will be in the front of the line for reward at the judgment seat of Christ. . . before a great many people I have met.

The day was ending, and the sun was beginning to set. The people began to make their way down the dirt path headed back home. It would be another seven hour walk for them, and they would be walking in the dark jungle till late that evening. The band had a Toyota minivan. The van was slightly larger than one you might see in America. They all piled into the van with their instruments, and then, several of them climbed onto the top of the van to sit on the roof. They then made their way down the dirt road with some of them playing their horns.

It was a sight to behold.

We were cracking up laughing as we imagined what would happen if we tried this in the States . . . but then again, if anyone had ever been in a church bus ministry . . . well.

TAKE NOTE SWIATKOWSKI

"But godliness with contentment is great gain. For we brought nothing into this world, and it is certain we can carry nothing out. And having food and raiment let us be therewith content. But they that will be rich fall into temptation and a snare, and into many foolish and hurtful lusts, which drown men in destruction and perdition" (1 Timothy 6:6-9).

The more a people are blessed, the less grateful they become.

While in Africa, I saw people who were so excited about the church and the opportunity to hear the word of God. They were willing to work hard to build a church; they were willing to walk for miles to dedicate a new church building; and they always put on their best clothes to go to church. They sang with all their heart, sat in a hot building with no AC, and nobody complained or moved. They were happy in Jesus. If we looked around, based on our standards in America, they lacked all the things we think are necessary to be happy.

It can be a struggle for Christians to learn to be content and be happy with what God has placed in their hands. God is not discouraging hard work and advancement, but He is warning us against greed and the dangers that come with it.

They Don't Make Marines Like They Used To

Once we were back at the mining camp, Brother Arnold went to his room and I went to mine. After the long day, I wanted nothing more than to get ready for bed. I was washing some of my things out in the sink when I heard a noise come from Brother Arnold's room. I heard a large thud, and then he yelled, "OOOOOH!"

There was another thud.

"OH! OOOOH GET OUT!" He yelled.

I stood there. . . afraid to move.

I thought, *"If he is getting killed, I'll stay here and wait for the assailant to come get me."*

"Matt, come help me!" he yelled.

I was thinking, *"I don't want to help you,"* but that's what I was there for, to help him. So, off I went.

When I entered his room, the mattress was hanging off the bed, the sheets and blankets were disheveled, and Brother Arnold stood, in the midst of it all, frightened.

"What's going on?" I asked.

"There was a lizard on my bed!" He answered while pointing at the mattress.

These lizards were small, were seen just about everywhere, and resembled a Gecko. We had seen some on our windows but on the outside. He was trying to get it but was afraid.

I started to look around the room for it.

"There he is! That little devil! Kill him. . . get him!" He shrieked, pointing at the lizard.

I grabbed a shoe and smacked that lizard silly.

Now, I'll be honest, I don't know if I killed it or knocked it unconscious, but it had stopped moving. So, I picked him up by the tail and threw him out the door. I walked back to the room. Brother Arnold was already putting his bed back together. He looked at me and started laughing.

"I thought you were a Marine," I said. "How in the world are you afraid of lizards?! You guys are supposed to storm beaches and stuff!"

"Well, I wasn't a good Marine," he said through his laughter.

We both stood there cracking up for a moment, and then I went back to my room laughing all the way. I closed my door ready to go to bed but not before quickly searching it and the rest of the room for lizards.

MONDAY

Visiting the Schools

It never ceases to amaze me how God can bless us even when our attitude stinks. It doesn't take much for our flesh to become riled. We often blame the Devil, but I'm pretty convinced it's nothing more than our sorry flesh.

I went to sleep that night happy and excited about what I had seen and been a part of, but in the middle of the night, I woke up thinking about my luggage. I started to grow angry. I then started thinking about the Health Care debate that was going on back in the States, and it began to get to me as well. The only television we could receive in the Africa mining camp was

Al-Jazeera, and it was very slanted and biased. But with no other options, we watched that before we went to bed.

My mind wondered back to my luggage. I thought for sure my luggage was stolen, and I would never see it again.

Now, some of you might be asking what the big deal about my luggage was? You are not the first person, and you won't be the last, to ask that question. Yep, I know it shouldn't have been such a big deal, but I was letting my flesh get the better of me.

The next day, we received a phone call from Brussels airline. They informed me that they had my luggage, and it would be in Freetown late Friday. I was relieved and thankful! I began to weep when I thought how faithless I had been, and yet, my God has been so good to me.

TAKE NOTE SWIATKOWSKI

God was my supply; I had not wanted anything. I had been able to alternate my clothing just fine, and I was able to wash some of the things in the bathroom sink and hang them up to dry in my room. I had not had to worry about dragging a suitcase across the countryside.

All of the foolishness on my part was me worrying about material possessions, in other words. . . just stuff. Everything on that trip had shown the faithfulness of God. How often I think of what a failure I am. I have seen Gods provide, and yet I doubt.

This was a simple mission's trip, and I was fretting over pants and shirts. But how often do so many of Gods people let such trivial things stop them from being successful in the work of Christ? It is always the small things that we stumble over. When there's a large object, we just break out the ropes and climbing gear and go to work, but the small, tiny things cause us to fall on our face.

"The young lions do lack and suffer hunger: but they that seek the LORD shall not want any good thing" (Psalm 34:10).

Our Worst Is Still Better

The next morning, we drove to the village of Mokunji to visit the Steve Ware High School as well as the Fagara Preparatory School. The high school was named after a very godly and dear friend who pastored in Orlando, Florida. Dr. Ware was, and continued to be, a faithful supporter of the work there and was very generous in so many ways.

The principal of the school was a good man by the name of Henry Pratt, and he was doing a fine job running things. The school was a complex of one-story buildings spread out over a large piece of land. The buildings had suffered from the ravages of war, and the scars were evident. There were doors that were broken or missing, there were windows with no glass in them. . . just empty openings, there were smashed walls, and many broken blackboards.

It was a sad sight.

But even with all of the damage, they were using these buildings, and young people were being educated. The high school ran about 176 students: 98 boys and 78 girls. The primary school, which was started by Mary Pratt, ran about 60 students: 24 boys and 36 girls. They were being taught in sad conditions, but to them, it was school. To be honest, they didn't know anything else because this was all they had seen or had ever known.

We made another trip, and this time, we went to the village of Njagbahun (pronounced Jaw-bon), which was the home of Max Gorvie. It was a long, hot drive to, what appeared to be, the middle of nowhere. This was one of the saddest villages I had ever seen. The village was made up of little, round mud huts with thatch roofs and hard clay floors. The people there were very thin, and many looked malnourished. The poverty there was beyond description. The children did not go to school after the third grade. It was hard to imagine that this was all they would ever know. Most would be born there, marry there, and die there. They would never see most of their country. . . let alone the world.

One little girl, around two years old, saw me and started crying. I usually have that effect on women, but this little girl was crying because she was scared. She had never seen a white man before. Her mother was holding her and laughing. Everyone around her was laughing as well.

We met with the elders of the village and walked with them. We saw the crops they were growing, and almost everyone wanted to say hello and talk to us as we made our way around the village. There was a small church that also served as the schoolhouse, and there was a small Muslim Mosque as well.

You would be hard pressed to find a place so poor and destitute in the US. We have so much, and yet, so many complain and gripe. I heard no complaining there in the midst of poverty. They mostly wanted help for a better education for their children.

We left and made the long drive back to the mining camp. We ate our meal and then retired for the night. Tomorrow, we would begin the long drive to the country of Liberia for a preachers' meeting and a revival meeting.

Chapter Ten

OFF TO BO

TUESDAY

We began the long drive to Bo, the second largest city in Sierra Leone. It would take about three hours to get there. The roads were all dirt, so we drove slowly (this was done to protect our tires from having a blowout).

When we arrived later, we would stop and spend the rest of the day there. The trip was pretty much uneventful, but we all had a good time conversing.

Chicken, Stitch, Freeze

When we arrived in town, I was not sure what to expect. Solomon and Marcel began to look around and compare Bo to Freetown, and in their assessment, they said Freetown was a much better place. They would do this comparison game again when we arrived at Monrovia in Liberia. I guess we all do this and compare other places to home.

It was now late afternoon, and we needed something to eat. So, we began to look for a restaurant that would cater to our taste. We found a nice, little restaurant; it served chicken and fries. The chicken was a rotisserie style with a nice seasoning, and it was quite good. We enjoyed ourselves (as well as the AC the restaurant provided).

After our meal, we made our way to where we would be staying. It was a small hotel, and as we entered the courtyard, we saw a small little café on the right side. A very nice lady ran the place. After talking to her, we discovered she was a Christian. All of the cooking was done on an open fire that she had going. She wanted us to eat, but we informed her we had just finished our supper. I could not get used to the idea that 99% of people in the country cooked on an open fire. It was how America would have done it one hundred years ago. The smell of smoke was in the air no matter where you went.

The landlady checked us into our rooms. It was all one level, and there were many different sized rooms. We each got a room to ourselves that was probably 7' by 10'. It had a bed, a dresser, a window, a TV, and an AC unit. There was a common bathroom down the hall which was definitely an upgrade from a hole in the ground.

After checking in, we decided to walk around town. As we made our way around, the seam of my pants ripped. I don't know why except to say that they were not the greatest quality. I was down to three pairs of pants.

"This is just great," I thought. *"Now what am I going to do?!"*

As if to further aggravate me, Brother Arnold had received a phone call from Brussels airlines informing me there was a short three-day strike. They could not be sure if my bag would arrive on Friday.

My flesh began to stir up within me again, and if I would have dwelt on the current situation with my luggage, I would have had a rotten time.

When my pants ripped, I asked Brother Arnold to walk behind me to see if he could see the tear.

"It's not noticeable," he said, waving me off.

I started to think that maybe he had said that just so I wouldn't be embarrassed or self-conscious. No sooner had he informed me of this fact than we walked a few hundred yards and saw a small tailor shop on the street. We asked the man if he could fix the seam and he said that he could.

Now, again, this was Africa and it was not a normal tailor shop. It was open in the front with a small table that he sewed on. Behind him was a room that he stored his items in. He told me to go behind the wall and hand him my trousers. The wall was only three feet high. So, from my waist up, I was visible to all on the street. I sat on a chair near me and watched the world go by as he worked on my pants.

"Praise God! This is amazing how God worked this out!" Brother Arnold was shouting.

I was sitting there with no pants, smiling, and nodding at people as they walked by staring at the white man making a scene. I had some strange thought cross my mind from time to time, as I sat there.

"Suppose this guy just takes off with my pants," I thought. *"Then what?"*

Then I thought, *"But why in the world would he run off with my pants? And what kind of person has these crazy thoughts? But if he did run off, then what would I do? I would be stuck back here. I guess I could grab some material he had stored here and wrap myself up. . ."*

No sooner had I started trying to banish those foolish thoughts than he had finished my pants and handed them off to me good as new. We paid the man and walked back to our hotel. The pants lasted the rest of the trip, and I never had a problem with them. If you are ever in Bo and need a good tailor, look for the short old guy. He will fix you right up.

It was very hot outside, and we worked up a great sweat that day. A good, long shower was in order, and after that, off to our rooms for a good night's rest. Once in my room, I took the only bag I had, a very small bag that carried my only possessions in the world at that moment and placed them in the top drawer of my dresser.

The AC was a wall unit and was blowing full blast. It was a large unit, probably twice the size of what was needed in the room.

I walked over to turn it down. All the knobs were missing and the shaft for the knob was so deeply recessed in the unit that I could not reach it with my fingers.

"Well," I thought, *"I will just have to unplug it, and when it gets warm, I can plug it back in."*

As I reached for the plug, I realized that someone had placed a metal strap across the plug and screwed it in so it could not be disconnected.

I looked for a circuit breaker in the room, but there wasn't one.

Now, you may be asking yourselves why I wouldn't just crawl under the covers in order to stay warm, but therein lay the problem. My bed had only one thin sheet on it, and it would not keep me warm as I was already freezing in the room.

It was at this point that I had a brilliant thought. I could open the window and let warm air in and some of the cold air out. The windows were the old crank out style and the handle was missing. As much as I tried, I could not turn the small knob by hand.

"If only I had my luggage, I would have warmer clothes and even my Leatherman tool kit, and I would be able to do something with the window," I thought miserably.

But I didn't have my luggage.

In the end, I put on my long pants and a couple of shirts and crawled under the sheet with my bath towel on top of me.

As I laid there shivering, I began to think of my wife Renee and my children. I sure did miss them and prayed they were doing well. I thought of them every day, and any time I saw families together, I thought of mine and what they might be doing at that same moment.

I learned that we are creatures of habit. We have our routines, and our family doesn't stray too much from it. So I always knew, or had a pretty good idea, what they were doing when I was thinking about them.

WEDNESDAY

In the morning, I got up and opened the door only to be hit with a humid heat wave that felt really good. As I stood there, I began to thaw out from the previous night.

We had a small breakfast and waited for Solomon to show up. They were constructing a new hotel on sight, and it was just a shell. Brother Arnold and

I decided to be adventurous. We walked around the hotel from floor to floor; we went into the rooms, and even made our way to the roof. It was several stories high, and from there we could get a good view of the city. Children saw us and started yelling to us and waving. We smiled back and waved. Solomon came along in search of us and eventually looked up and saw us. He laughed. We went down to join him and were on our way.

The city of Bo was a large city, but sadly, the cults had been very busy in deceiving the people there. The Mormons and the Watchtower association had congregations all over the city . . . and then there was the Muslim influence. All of these false religions were keeping many people in darkness, as well as the outright voodoo and witchcraft that went on.

It was certainly ripe for someone to work full-time giving the people of Bo the true bread of life.

PHOTO ALBUM

Breakfast on the First Day

The Airport at Lungi

The Garbage Field

Sitting Three to Four to a Desk

School Under the Tree

Preaching in Liberia

Machete Man

The Children Love to Have Their Photo Taken

Dr. Arnold with the Handicapped Man

Church in Texas

Beautiful John O Bay

Dr. Arnold at the New Testament School

Giant Ant Hill in Williams Town

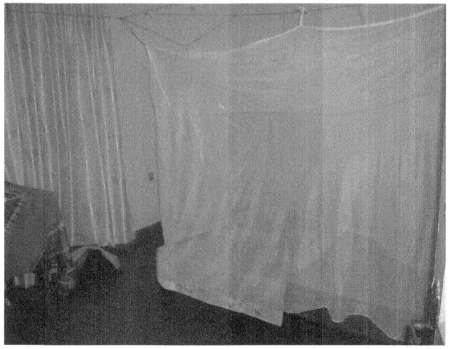

My Bed with Mosquito Netting

The Lunch Lady at School

Dr. Arnold in the Hammock

In Williams Town with the Items I Purchased in Africa

The Pineapple Stand at the Barge

The Godless Rooster

Young Man with a Rat

Chapter Eleven

WEDNESDAY CONTINUED

Ants, Barges, and Crocodiles

We started the long drive to Liberia early the next morning. All along the way the roads were rough and winding. There were few villages as we drove. One thing that I found of great interest was the Rubber Tree forest we drove through. I was amazed when I saw it and wished we had time to stop. It was quite unique as all the trees were lined up in rows; you could tell that they were planted by someone years earlier. They were tall, thin trees that were so different from anything else I had seen up to that point. The road was cut right through the middle of the forest, and on either side was the rubber tree forest. On our return trip, we had more time to stop and go exploring the natural wonder, but not on the way.

In order to get to Liberia, we had to cross the river Zimmi. The map called it the Mano River, but Zimmi was what Solomon called it, so we went with the locals. At the village of Jaiwulo, which was by the river, there was no bridge. . . just an old barge system that they pulled across with ropes and cables. When we arrived at the village, the barge had just pulled away, and it would take a good 30 minutes to return to us.

While we were there, we discovered that they had an up and running local McDonalds. Well, not really. It was four bamboo poles in the ground with palm leaves for a roof. Under the roof there was a large black kettle. The ladies were cooking fish for the travelers. We were informed that we should not eat the fish as it might make us sick. I was getting a little hungry, but with that information, I thought I could wait for supper later on.

Solomon, his dad, Max, and Marcel walked over to the pot of fish and ordered some. I was watching them eat. There was very little waste going on between them. They would stick the fish in their mouth and eat away, only stopping to spit out some bones. They even sucked on the tail of that thing!

I must have had a strange expression on my face because Solomon looked at me and said, "In Africa, we don't waste anything."

Then Solomon pointed out that there was a man selling fresh pineapple. He cut it up right there in front of us and placed it in plastic bags. That was the best tasting pineapple I have ever had in my life.

I sat down by the side of the road and noticed a black line going across it, which appeared to be moving. I got closer and saw that it was a large colony of ants all moving across the road.

"What in the world were they doing?" I thought.

I sat there and ate my pineapple while staring at the ants. I began to wonder if they were the killer ants I had heard so much about back home.

"Solomon, are these killer ants?!" I asked in alarm.

"No, Matt. They're just regular ants," he said after smiling and laughing at my assumption.

Some of the juice from my pineapple dripped onto the ground where the ants were, and they flocked to the spot. I dropped a small piece of pineapple for them and watched as they carried it off. It was fascinating how they all worked together to accomplish the task at hand.

Just about then, the barge returned, and Marcel (the driver) drove the vehicle on board. I remember thinking how cool it was that we got to ride on the barge.

"So, Matt. Have you ever seen how they call crocodiles here?" Brother Arnold asked.

"No, I don't think I have," I responded.

I was curious to see how it was done. He approached the rails of the barge and looked out over the river. He then placed his hands to the sides of his mouth.

"Heeeeeere crocodile, heeeeere crocodile, crocodile, crocodile!" He cried out with a loud, high-pitched voice.

Everyone, including the barge workers, began laughing, and so did I. We made it to the other side of the river and began our journey to Bo.

Oh, and no crocodiles ever emerged.

TAKE NOTE SWIATKOWSKI

"Go to the ant, thou sluggard; consider her ways, and be wise" (Proverbs 6:6).

"The ants are a people not strong, yet they prepare their meat in the summer" (Proverbs 30:25).

God created all things.

He designed the ants to do what they do. I saw the handy work of my God in those tiny creatures as they worked together to carry food (including large chunks of pineapple). Now if God, in His Word, instructs us to look at the ants, then the best thing we can do is look at the ants. The ants prepare for the future, yet man, in all his wisdom, does so little thinking about his future. Some think this is untrue because we prepare for retirement with pensions and such; however, I am not referring to our earthly future but instead to our eternal future, the one that waits for all people. Too many individuals hope or think that by their good virtues they will be a shoo-in for heaven. Yet, they never read what the God of heaven says about good works and Heaven, or how He says they can go there. Many take the word of spiritual leaders and follow them blindly. Then there are those who use the Bible but let their leader interpret it for them. They don't spend time reading the instructions themselves. The Bereans were wise because they studied the scriptures to see if the Apostle Paul was telling it straight or not.

Check, Check, Check, Check, Check, and Check

From our location, it was short drive to the country of Liberia, and once again, we had to cross a river to get into the country. Just on the other side of the bridge was a checkpoint. We had to provide all our passports and visas as well as proper documentations for the vehicle. They searched the car thoroughly. Then, they made us all get out of the car and searched us.

After being searched and returning to the car, we made a quick left and drove a hundred yards to another, much larger, check point. It was complete with a police department, jail, and all the other things necessary to scare foreigners.

We all knew we would be there for a while. We got out of the car again and made our way into the building. We provided our paperwork, and then, we were given a tour of the lovely facility. They were all brown buildings, and they were all very old and in poor shape. This country had also been affected by the war that ravaged Sierra Leone.

As the officer was leading us down a long hallway, he pointed out a jail cell to us.

"We put bad people in here."

I thought, *"Well, that's normally where they go."*

"Not to worry. I'm a good guy!" I said.

He didn't seem amused.

The door to the jail cell was made of steel with a small window at the top that had steel bars. I looked inside the opening, and the stench hit me hard!

It was the smell of human urine.

There was no toilet facility for prisoners and no beds. The walls had old paint on them that was faded and peeling. Some old person had scratched in the paint the words "Help me Jesus". I knew, if I were in there, I would probably have written the same thing. I quickly moved on from the prison door.

We sat around for over an hour because they were not happy with the documentation for the car.

I leaned over to talk to Solomon.

"What's wrong?" I asked.

"Nothing is wrong," he whispered. "They just want money."

He was not going to give them a dime, and so, they made us wait. I'm sure if we had slipped them something, we would have been out of there in fifteen minutes.

We finally got the green light and drove out of the driveway. We proceeded another hundred yards only to have another check point. The three check points were in the shape of a U. They could clearly see each other and could even yell to each other.

"Why don't you just yell to the other guys and ask if we are ok?" I asked check point Charlie.

Again, I was met with another man in the country with no sense of humor.

We didn't stay long and were once again on our way. We had to stop at check points three more times. At one stop, they made us get out of the car and wait in a little roadside hut. I noticed a picture on the wall and knew the man was familiar to me. It was a white man, obviously, an American with clothes that dated back over one hundred and fifty years. I asked Brother Arnold and the other men who he was, but they didn't know.

Finally, the guard came back.

"Who is the man in the picture?" I asked.

"He is the prophet, Joseph Smith," he answered.

Smith was the founder of the cult called Mormonism.

"Are you a practicing Mormon?" I asked.

"Yes, I am," he answered.

He left us again, but this time, Solomon went with him and soon returned.

"What's going on?" we asked Solomon.

"He wants money, but I told him none was coming," he informed us.

Eventually, the guard let us go on our way.

The Coastal Capital

With all the check points behind us, we made our way to Monrovia. The city had an interesting history and was named after American President James Monroe. Founded in 1822, President Monroe was a prominent supporter of sending freed Black slaves and ex-Caribbean slaves from the United States of America and the Caribbean islands to Liberia. He saw it as preferable to emancipation in America. This idea might offend and anger many today. I don't think it was the right idea, but it was done, and now the capitol city bears his name.

While we were there, we were looking for the pastor who would be hosting the preachers meeting. We were told that he would be by a bridge. I thought that was odd, but to date, not much had been normal. Sure enough, we came to the bridge he had told us about, and there he was. There was a lady with him who, apparently, had some pull. I soon discovered that these two countries are heavy on the matriarchal.

Pastor Mulba Kallon was a short man who was led to Christ many years earlier in Sierra Leone. He was part of the refugee movement as they were fleeing the rebels during the war. He had started several churches, and the meeting we were having was to be at a place they called the Chicken Soup Baptist Church. I had to ask a few times about that name. It turned out that the community had taken the name from the now defunct Maggi Bouillon Cube Factory (pronounced Magee) that was once there. When the war started, the company pulled out and never came back. Maggi's products can be seen in many grocery stores, well, at least where I live.

We stopped in town to get a bite to eat, and all I can say is that I was hungry after eating only pineapple. I got a hamburger, and basically, it only helped to keep me alive. The fellowship was good, and I enjoyed getting to meet and talk with pastor Kallon.

We had started on our way to the Chicken Soup Church, but traffic was a nightmare. I had thought NY was bad until I saw Freetown, and this was far worse than Freetown. People and cars were everywhere. It was a logistical nightmare, and I was glad I didn't have to drive through it.

Book 'em Danno!

We arrived at the soup factory, and sure enough, there was a large wall behind the old, abandoned factory with the words "Maggi" written on it. This was going to be an open-air meeting, and I was the only preacher on the schedule.

It was dark out, and when it's nighttime in Africa, it gets very dark. There were no (or very few) streetlights and not many other lights emanating from the cities. You couldn't see very many stars at night because the smoke from the fires used for cooking hangs low in the sky.

I was exhausted as the day's events had worn on me, and I barely had any energy left for preaching. When the day was blazing hot and there wasn't any relief from the heat, it drains you of energy. I was excited to preach to them and tell them about Jesus, but I needed the Lord to help. We preachers often say that we need the Lord. What we really mean is that we need the Lord all of the time, not only when we are tired, but also when we feel good.

Preaching needs the hand of God on it, or it will all be vain.

The service started with what, I guess, was supposed to be music and special singing. To be honest, it was bad. It sounded like a cat dying a slow death and letting everyone know about it. Even the music was just noise! I tried to ask the Lord to help me with it but to no avail.

The courtyard was packed with people, and it was really hard to tell how many were there. They told me it was over 1000 people. To date, that was the largest crowd I have ever preached to.

There I was . . . feeling bad again because I was wearing a Hawaiian styled short sleeve shirt. It was blue with yellow tropical flowers on it. I had bought the little beauty in the markets in Freetown. I thought we would change before the service, but there was no time for any of that. Nobody had a problem with me wearing the shirt, but the African preachers were dressed up. I felt like I looked like a reject from *Hawaii Five O*.

The area was very dimly lit with a string of lights hanging around the pulpit area, and it was difficult to see. But the Lord helped me as I knew my message. I was trying to feel the leading of the blessed Spirit of God directing me. I also had to preach through an interpreter, and again, it was very difficult for me. You say a sentence and he repeats it, say another sentence, and he repeats it. He was not that fluent in the English language, but I knew he was far better in English than I was in his Liberian dialect.

I preached and then gave the invitation for those who didn't know Christ to be saved. There is no way to say how many came to know Christ that night, I left that to the Lord and did my part to help those who said they prayed and asked for salvation. After the preaching, I thought they would all go home . . . at least that's what happens in America.

Much to my surprise, they all stayed. They sang gospel songs for hours afterwards. When nothing remains to steal one's time and the country has suffered the effects of war, maybe one feels the need to grow closer to the Lord. That's what they were doing. It was certainly something I was not familiar with. At home, while at our church, people hung around for a while after service and fellowshipped with each other, which is great, but never had I seen in any church people pick up again and start praising the Lord.

TAKE NOTE SWIATKOWSKI

"Then he answered and spake unto me, saying, This is the word of the LORD unto Zerubbabel, saying, Not by might, nor by power, but by my spirit, saith the LORD of hosts" (Zechariah 4:6).

One thing that is hard for preachers to learn is their absolute reliance on the Lord when preaching. Preachers often give lip service to that thought, yet somehow, we think if we communicate clearly, if our delivery is perfect, if all the points fit, and the little humor adds the right touch throughout, well then, we think it was good.

There is another line preachers like to use and it is, "I had liberty in preaching." While it is important to be the best we can be, it is also important to never forget that God doesn't need any of that.

When I was very new in the pastorate, I thought I had a good sermon one day, but as soon as I started preaching, it went south real fast. I mean, I could not wait to be finished because it was so bad. I was fifteen minutes in and wanted to quit. I felt ashamed to quit so soon, and so, I kept dragging that dead corpse of a sermon for another fifteen minutes. I was thoroughly ashamed and discouraged by the end. I had everyone stand and pray. Silently, I prayed in my shame to the Lord and said, *"Let me see you do something with that Lord."*

I didn't say it with sarcasm but with total humiliated and discouraged self. I can't describe it except to say that God showed up. People came forward, there was crying, and it was a mini revival. People didn't leave, they stayed there praying. I stood there not knowing what to do. One man told me, "Pastor, that was the worst sermon you ever preached, but God showed up."

I said yes it was, and yes, He did.

The Lord showed me that He just needs a surrendered vessel, and He can work. He doesn't need my "A" game. I was reminded in Africa, though tired, sluggish, and using an interpreter, that I need God, and the people needed God. . . they didn't need me. Yet, this truth has been repeated time and time again, and the Lord still reminds me that it's all Him and not me.

This Is Where I Die

The time had come. I needed to use the restroom. We were in a compound that looked like it was bombed out, and it had been bombed out. I whispered to the preacher asking if there was a restroom nearby. I did this as discreetly as possible. He then turned around and yelled out in his native tongue. Several people, including ladies, all came running. They took me into a block building that was burnt out. There was a small candle to light the way, and they led me down a dark hallway. They took a right turn into a darker hallway, then a left turn into an even darker hallway. There was debris on the floor that I could feel as I walked but had trouble seeing. I had two thoughts the whole time:

First: *"It's not possible for it to get darker with each turn we make."*

Second: *"Well, I always wondered where I was going to die, and now I know."*

Eventually, we came to a door. Inside I could hardly see. I was squinting the whole time. I briefly thought that if I had my luggage, I would have had a flashlight. There was a window in the room that provided some light, and from what I could see, there was a toilet bowl. This was obviously a bathroom once upon a time. Now, it was just a toilet bowl. Just a bowl . . . no tank. They said something to me before they left, but I couldn't understand them.

At that point, I didn't need to go anymore. So, I just stood there in the dark room with half a toilet trying to figure out how to find my way out of there. A few moments later, there was banging on the door, which startled me. I reached over where I was sure the door was and opened it halfway ready to slam it shut just in case something bad happened. There was a group of people all yelling and handing me a bucket of water. I took the bucket and said thank you. I closed the door and just stood there. I didn't have the heart to tell them that the moment had passed. After all, they had put so much effort into getting me in there. I waited, poured the water into the toilet, and then opened the door. I looked around but didn't see anybody.

"Hello, anybody there?" I said sheepishly.

There was a young man waiting for me, but I didn't see him until he spoke up. He scared the daylights out of me. He led me back outside and was informed that we would be leaving even though they were still singing.

Hotel Please

We left the meeting, and to this day, I am not sure if there was a hotel planned or not. We drove through the crowds at night, and for the first time, I was a little nervous for our safety. In fact, I could sense a very strong demonic presence. Some may think I was crazy, but spiritual battles are real, and the hair on the back of my neck was standing up. I reminded myself that this was a country given to idolatry and false religion, which was evident by the show of Mormonism.

We came to one place, and I didn't like the way it looked. I prayed that it was not going to be our hotel. We drove a little farther and came to another hotel. The Lord gave me some peace and seemed to tell me that this was where we would stay, and we would be safe.

We made our way inside. The hotel was clean, and the staff was friendly. We were provided the keys to our room and made our way upstairs. We each had our own room, and it was large and clean. I even had my own bathroom! This was the first time since arriving in Africa that I had a bathroom all to myself. Honestly, it's the little things that make the difference.

I started not to feel well around this time, but thankfully, after a few hours, the medicine Renee packed for me helped, and I was eventually able to get a good night's sleep with no further issues.

THURSDAY

Teaching, Rice, and Junk Luggage

We woke up early the next morning and had a nice breakfast in the hotel dining area. The lady who worked there was expecting a baby. We had a pleasant conversation with her. She talked about her faith in the Lord Jesus. She expressed concern over the health of her baby and started crying. She wanted us to pray for her. We did this gladly, and as we left for the day, her fears seemed to subside.

We made our way back to the Chicken Soup area to have the preachers meeting. After what I had seen the night before, I was convinced that there were some good men there. They simply lacked proper training. They were doing their best with what little knowledge they had, but it can be dangerous for the people to have leadership that does not have their own biblical convictions in order.

The meeting was packed. Not only were there preachers, but also Christian schoolteachers. Many women teachers were there, and they all stayed for the preaching and teaching sessions. Max Gorvie spoke and so did Solomon, Brother Arnold, and I.

Before the trip, I was informed about this meeting, and I was to have print outs ready. I did have them. As a matter of fact, I had dozens of handouts, but they were in my MIA suitcase. I had everything on my computer back home. I had thought about asking my wife to email them to Solomon, but using email and finding a printer was nearly an impossible task. So, with no handouts, I tried to remember my subject matter offhand, and I presented my message.

During the trip, I had been working on my outline and trying to get all of my points in order from memory. I also asked my Father if I should do something different. But He gave me wisdom and helped me to get my message together. Spiritual battles are real, and again, I was letting myself get aggravated about not having my stuff with me. To add to my frustration, all the other preachers had their handouts and were dressed in their Sunday best. Once again, I was stuck wearing a polo and Khakis. I taught my lesson and asked them to take notes. To be honest, I felt like a failure when I was done. The other men seemed to have things flowing, and God was on them.

I kept thinking, *"Why did I even bother?"*

The ladies had food prepared for our lunch break, but most of it was, once again, not suitable for us. They had a large yellow bucket, the kind you would use to carry laundry in with the rope handles on the sides. This was filled halfway with fish. One might think that it would not be bad, but let me explain. They cut the fish in half (not long ways but width ways where the two pieces were the tail end or the head end). The head end still had the eyes in them, and I am not a big fan of eating things that are looking at me. They would take this, put it in a big cauldron, add seasonings and spices, and boil it. When it was done cooking, they would all go to town eating the fish. They would even suck on the tail end of it.

The only thing suitable for us was some white rice. I was hungry, so I ate it. Growing up, we never ate much rice, and if we did, we had a bottle of La Choy soy sauce nearby. My father was strictly a meat and potatoes man. Once I asked him why he didn't eat rice, and he responded with, "I fought a war against them people."

He was referring to the Japanese. He was a WWII vet.

Now understand, I like to eat rice; however, it's not on my top ten favorite food list. I was hungry though, and rice was available. When you're hungry, there's nothing like a good bowl of white rice. I was really hoping for some plain white crackers to compliment the meal, but alas there weren't any.

After they gave out the rice, I jokingly asked for some soy sauce. The ladies just looked at each other and then at me. I tried to explain it was a joke, but it went over badly.

One lady ran to ask people for soy sauce.

"Never mind! I was only joking!" I yelled after her.

She didn't listen and told me to wait as she ran away. This was one of those times when I would say to myself, "Matt, just learn to keep your mouth shut."

I walked away and had started eating my rice when the dear lady found me. She was a sweet, Christian woman who was also an albino. She told me that they couldn't find what I was looking for.

I thanked her for her kindness, and then I sat there feeling foolish.

We saw a little market, and I was glad when Brother Arnold said we'd go over and get some pineapple. The man cut up the pineapple and gave it to us. It was beyond delicious.

Never in my life have I tasted pineapple like the ones I had in Africa. I was hooked on them and looked for every opportunity while there to obtain some. Now, one thing I'm not proud of is my knowledge of pineapples. To be honest, I never gave them much thought before going to Africa. As far as I was concerned, they came in a can in varieties of ways: crushed, chunked, sliced, or the ones I saw whole in the grocery store. I always liked them and even drank pineapple juice, but I never thought about how they grew.

You see, I'm from New Jersey, so we don't grow these bad boys around there. If you want to talk tomatoes, blueberries, cranberries, and/or corn well, we can talk. . . but not pineapples.

When I went to visit my Aunt Louisa and Uncle Richard in Florida back in 1998, I was excited to see a grapefruit tree. I knew they grew on trees, but I had never seen one before in person. When it came to pineapples, I had never thought about where they came from. I had never been anywhere where they grew them. . . until Africa. On the trip, when I saw a pineapple bush, I was in shock and amazement.

"Look! It's a pineapple, and it's growing on a bush!" I said excitedly.

"Yes. Where did you think they came from?" They all asked me.

"I don't know," I shrugged defensively. "I never gave it a moment's thought. Maybe, if I had, I would have thought: on a tree."

After all, you have coconut trees so there must be pineapple trees. It never dawned on me to think of a bush. How amazed and thrilled I was to see one.

The day was extremely hot, so much so that the African people were complaining. I was drenched with sweat, and I was thankful that at least I had deodorant. My all-day ordeal in the U.S., and then the long flight to Brussels had been so stressful that I had needed deodorant. I had, what I liked to call, "Union" deodorant because it quit working after eight hours. When we landed in Brussels, I had run to the bathroom to apply a fresh batch. In Africa, I was sure to keep a fresh supply on at all times, even though many in the country had no idea what deodorant was. I never said a word to them because, to be honest, they were more concerned with where the next meal was coming from and didn't have time for trivial things like deodorant.

We finished our food, had a short meeting, and then went back to the hotel.

While we were sitting in the horrendous traffic on the way back to the hotel, I noticed men selling luggage and soft bags. They were right there on the street and would come up to the cars to ask if you wanted anything. This caught my eye because the bag I was using for my clothes was good when I left home because it only contained a small number of items, but now that I was using it to carry the extra supplies of clothes and extra stuff, it was too small.

I asked Solomon to ask the man how much. They began to barter while we sat in the car and inched down the road. They haggled for a good 20 minutes while we traveled a total of about 20 feet.

Yep, we were tearing up pavement around there.

I was able to buy a lager, black bag that would fit everything I had nicely (including my original bag) all for the sum of ten American dollars.

Now, my mom always said that you get what you pay for, and sure enough, a ten-dollar bag was a ten-dollar bag. By Saturday, the zipper would break on the piece of junk. It was the long zipper. So, when it broke, the bag was almost split in two and good for nothing. I had to go back to my original bag. I never told my wife this story because, if I did, she would have asked if I went back to Liberia to get my money back or if I used a coupon for my purchase. Praise the Lord for wives and all the money they save with coupons as well as all the other deals they figure out.

Once back at the hotel, we got cleaned up, rested, and had our meal. We all knew that tomorrow would be a very long day as we headed back to Freetown.

TAKE NOTE SWIATKOWSKI

"Now while Paul waited for them at Athens, his spirit was stirred in him, when he saw the city wholly given to idolatry" (Act 17:16).

In Liberia, although many Christians lived there, I still felt a presence of evil that I hadn't had, or felt, before. There were all kinds of false worship going on. . . evil worship. Just to be clear, if we are not worshiping the God of the Bible, it's false worship, and we are worshiping devils.

In scripture, Athens was given to false gods, but there is no God except the Lord himself. So, Paul knew what he was up against. The Bible tells us that Satan is the god of this world, and people are blinded by him. The man at the check point was under the false teaching that Joseph Smith was a prophet and will sit at the judgment seat with God the Father and Jesus. However, that's not scripture. Others in Liberia were involved in spiritism, voodoo, and so many other errors.

Biblical Christianity is the only thing that will help a nation rise from poverty, all other forms only enslave and keep it suppressed. My heart went out to the pastors there, as I knew they had a very large battle to fight. But that didn't stop them from trying to win souls and reach as many as they could with the saving Gospel of Jesus Christ.

Chapter Twelve

FREETOWN OR BUST

FRIDAY

Monkeys, Machete Man, and More Chicken

We left Liberia and made our way back to Freetown. It was eight o'clock when we left, and we would not get there until nine that night. It was a long, hot, and bumpy drive. The vast majority of it was back on the clay roads filled with weaving and swerving to avoid potholes and other things.

This type of traveling begins to wear on you after a while.

Once we were back on the barge, I was able to see some large monkeys swinging around in the trees. I learned a valuable lesson while watching those monkeys.

Most of us are all familiar with birds and what they often do as they fly by. We, our cars, or even our friends have been victims of their fly by . . . well . . . droppings.

I had never thought about monkeys though.

I made my way into the jungle looking up the whole time. As I was standing under a huge tree looking up, I heard a large sound crashing against the jungle floor. Curious, I walked over and found a large pile of monkey doo. The last thing I wanted was to be victimized so far from any place where I could wash up. So, I quickly realized that standing under the trees was not wise and made a hasty retreat to the road. I failed to pass this wisdom onto my comrades as I thought it was probably common knowledge for the locals.

When we got on the barge, I tried my hand at crocodile calling.

None appeared.

I guess I need more practice. After we reached the other side of the water, we headed down the road.

We continued driving and made our way back to the Rubber tree forest. It was an unusual sight to behold. We stopped the car to get out and look around. There was a man working, and when he saw us stop and get out, he disappeared. It was like that grainy Bigfoot video you see on the internet. He was looking at us, swinging his arms side to side with a machete, and then he was gone. We looked around for him, but he had just disappeared.

"Where did he go?" I asked.

"He left," Solomon said.

Sometimes people give you an answer that makes you just shake your head.

"I know he left, but why?"

"He must have been afraid."

"Afraid! He is the one with the machete," I thought.

I was afraid and was looking for him at every turn. I imagined him emerging from the jungle, screaming and swinging that machete, and me screaming, running down the road.

The trees all reached towards the heavens and lined up in perfect rows. Near the bottom of the trees there were small buckets. You could see where the tree had been cut at a 22 to 33-degree angle starting high on the left of the tree down to the right. There was a white liquid that ran down the length of the cut and into the bucket. The liquid's color and consistency resembled milk. As we looked at it, I decided to do something foolish: I dipped the tip of my finger into the white liquid. If you are ever near rubber trees, do not do this. My soul! It is a stink you can't believe! That monkey doo was better, and just like you would think, it was rubbery.

Have you ever done something and wondered seconds later just what you were thinking?

Well, that was me.

I was trying to figure out how to clean the white gunk off of my hand and get rid of the smell. I felt like that old man in the 1950s movie, *The Blob*. I had the substance on me, and I was sure I was going to get swallowed up by it.

Then, out of nowhere, machete man reappeared. I turned, and there he was. He was wearing a wool, brown hat, an oversized brown polo shirt, blue shorts with white trim, and was holding the machete. We said hello, and the men in our group started talking to the worker in their dialect.

He turned out to be very nice. He told us how to cut the tree and how the whole process worked. He told us that whatever we did, try not get the white liquid on us. Everyone turned and looked at me. I just smiled. I was using grass, roots, and leaves to clean my finger . . . occasionally smelling it.

Yep, it still stunk!

All in all, we spent a good hour there with him just looking and talking. We said goodbye and thanked him for showing us how he did his job. I don't think I will ever forget that man.

We hopped back in the car and made our way to Bo. Brother Arnold and I stopped back at the same restaurant. The other men in the group would eat somewhere else a little cheaper and more to their diet. After we had finished eating and rested a little bit, we continued our long journey to Freetown. We talked and slept in turn, but I was so glad to see that part of the world one more time.

TAKE NOTE SWIATKOWSKI

"Ah Lord GOD! Behold, thou hast made the heaven and the earth by thy great power and stretched out arm, and there is nothing too hard for thee" (Jeremiah 32:17).

I saw many aspects of God's creation from my flight across the Atlantic to my flight down from Europe to Africa. Then there were the many things I was blessed to see up close and personal. There was so much to see on the trip, and I didn't want to miss anything. The rubber tree forest, fresh pineapple and coconuts, the beautiful mountains and rain forests, the rivers, and the monkeys. They were all made by the hand of God. How good is our God that he made all of this for us to enjoy?! Oh, how He loves and provides all of this for us, and then, He gave us salvation through Christ.

How can anyone say there is no God, or that He does not care? Some point out all the suffering and ask how a loving God could do/allow that? My friends, understand that much of the world's suffering could be cured were it not for the greed of man. There is enough food and water to go around, yet man will keep it from fellow man, or he becomes too lazy and waits for others to do it for him. To be fair, there are things out of man's control that only God can fix. Someday, He will fix all things and right all wrongs when He returns. But until then, we live in a sin cursed creation, but God has taken and solved man's greatest need and that is the forgiveness of sin through Jesus Christ.

Welcome to the Kingdom

It was dark outside and getting late (already after nine). We were all exhausted and aching in our bones. I thought we were going back to the mission housing where we had stayed earlier, but they had no rooms available. Apparently, there was no plan for lodging after arriving.

We went to a hotel in town, but it was full. I was glad because it looked a little rough. Solomon suggested Family Kingdom, the hotel with the restaurants out front. As we drove to the hotel, Brother Arnold informed us that although it would be expensive, it was safe and clean. Fortunately, they were not full, and we were able to book our rooms. They had, what we would call, a suite. There were two bedrooms, two baths, and a small kitchen. Solomon went home to his wife, and Brother Max went back to the guest house.

The rooms were very nice and very clean. I have stayed in many hotels in America, and I couldn't help but notice all the things they did differently in Africa. Nothing strange, but there were some minor differences. Being a plumber, I tend to look at such things wherever I go. I noticed the slight styles along with some other things. Again, it's hard to describe, but you would know it was a room in a different country if you were to find yourself there. Not better and not worse, just different.

We were tired.

It was late after we checked in, so there was minimal talking. We went to our rooms in hopes of getting a good night's sleep.

SATURDAY

Why Is There Suffering?

The next morning, we made our way downstairs to an open courtyard. Under a large awning with openings on three sides, we had our breakfast. Each guest was allowed two eggs cooked any way they like them and as much fruit and breads as they liked. There was hot tea and coffee as well as fruit juices. It was a good breakfast. As we sat in the courtyard, out of the corner of my eye, I saw a small deer.

"What was that?" I thought to myself.

I strained to see if my eyes had deceived me, but sure enough, there was a small deer running around. It was part of the Kingdom, and it would roam around trying to mooch a meal at breakfast. It would even come up to people and let them pet it.

Today was supposed to be a day of rest, so after breakfast, we got changed to go swimming. The Family Kingdom sat right on the ocean. We could walk out the front gates, across the street, and the beach and ocean were right there.

I was glad to jump in the ocean and cool off.

There was a large group of young people at the beach that day, mostly children. Many of them wore no clothes because they were orphans. As soon as we dipped in, they began yelling.

"Hey white man," they called as they flocked around us.

"Why are you here in Africa? Are you here for diamonds or gold?" they asked.

We explained that we were preachers, and we were there to tell people about Jesus.

I had a small group of children around me, and there was a group around Brother Arnold as well.

A Muslim man came as well, and he began asking questions.

"If your God is so merciful, why does He allow suffering?" he asked.

Brother Arnold took him aside and was with him for quite some time trying to help him understand. I personally think the man didn't care if he received an answer or not; he was looking for an argument or a chance to win one.

We got cleaned up, but Brother Arnold was not feeling well. He had been having some issues with his colon. There was a doctor's office next to the Family Kingdom, so he paid him a visit. The doctor was a Lebanese man and seemed to be a good man who cared. He gave him some medication to help Brother Arnold feel better.

After visiting the doctor, we went to the restaurant in the middle of the courtyard. We sat under a large awning at a table with a large umbrella over it. From there, we could see the ocean just a few hundred yards away. We ate a small snack while we enjoyed the view. They served peanuts just like you get back home; we were also given a bottle of orange soda to drink. It was a relaxing and enjoyable time. After we had rested for a bit, we left to go and get cleaned up and ready for the evening.

While I was in my room, we received a phone call from Brussels airline.

They had my luggage.

"Where is it at?" I asked.

"In Brussels," they responded.

"Don't send it! Just leave it there, and I will pick it up on Tuesday morning when I arrive," I told them.

I was so relieved and happy. I was having a good time. I trusted that my luggage had enjoyed its vacation as well, and when I saw it on Tuesday, we could look at each other's vacation pics.

TAKE NOTE SWIATKOWSKI

As I think on those children we were swimming with and all they had been through, I thought of an age-old question. Why do the good suffer and the bad prosper? This is a question that people have asked the Lord for millenniums. The Psalmist asked this question of God in Psalm 73, and I think it says it better than any response I could give.

"A Psalm of Asaph. Truly God is good to Israel, even to such as are of a clean heart.   But as for me, my feet were almost gone; my steps had well-nigh slipped.   For I was envious at the foolish, when I saw the prosperity of the wicked.   For there are no bands in their death: but their strength is firm.   They are not in trouble as other men; neither are they plagued like other men.   Therefore pride compasseth them about as a chain; violence covereth them as a garment.   Their eyes stand out with fatness: they have more than heart could wish.   They are corrupt, and speak wickedly concerning oppression: they speak loftily.   They set their mouth against the heavens, and their tongue walketh through the earth.   Therefore his people return hither: and waters of a full cup are wrung out to them.   And they say, How doth God know? and is there knowledge in the most High?   Behold, these are the ungodly, who prosper in the world; they increase in riches.   Verily I have cleansed my heart in vain, and washed my hands in innocence.   For all the day long have I been plagued and chastened every morning.   If I say, I will speak thus; behold, I should offend against the generation of thy children.   When I thought to know this, it was too painful for me; Until I went into the sanctuary of God; then understood I their end.   Surely thou didst set them in slippery places: thou castedst them down into destruction.   How are they brought into desolation, as in a moment! they are utterly consumed with terrors.   As a dream when one awaketh; so, O

Lord, when thou awakest, thou shalt despise their image. Thus my heart was grieved, and I was pricked in my reins. So foolish was I, and ignorant: I was as a beast before thee. Nevertheless I am continually with thee: thou hast holden me by my right hand. Thou shalt guide me with thy counsel, and afterward receive me to glory. Whom have I in heaven but thee? and there is none upon earth that I desire beside thee. My flesh and my heart faileth: but God is the strength of my heart, and my portion forever. For, lo, they that are far from thee shall perish: thou hast destroyed all them that go a whoring from thee. But it is good for me to draw near to God: I have put my trust in the Lord GOD, that I may declare all thy works" (Psalm 73:1-28).

Best Chinese Food Ever

Growing up, we never ate Chinese food. My dad was strictly a meat and potatoes kinda guy with some Spaghetti and meatballs thrown in every now and again. On occasion, Mom would cook Dad short ribs, and we would have shrimp chow mein from a can along with white rice, and some crunchy La Choy Chinese noodles (also from a can).

When I was 22 years old, my coworker, Dave (I could write a book about our exploits together in the plumbing and heating trade) recommended that we get Chinese food for lunch. I got a little nervous because I had never ordered from a Chinese restaurant before. We went to a local take out place, and I stood there staring at the menu board with no clue as to what I was looking at. It was the same feeling I had when another friend took me to Starbucks for the first time. In fact, I have been back to Starbucks on many occasions, and I still have no idea what I'm looking at. I didn't know a General Tso from a moo goo gai pan, but Dave explained things to me. I ordered chicken lo mien and enjoyed it!

When I got married, I learned that my wife loved Chinese food, and she introduced me to more varieties. In fact, she worked as a waitress in one of the best Chinese restaurants I have ever been to. It was a little place in

Waycross, GA called Wong's Palace. Paul Tang and his wife left NYC to begin a simpler life and to start a restaurant. Now, being from Jersey, there are more Chinese restaurants than you can count. Please, no cat jokes. We have eaten a fair share at these restaurants. One of my favorites is called Lee's located in Lyndhurst.

Now, back in Africa, I was told we were going to a Chinese restaurant for dinner. I thought that it would be good, but to be honest, my expectations were low. After all, I was in Africa, and I hadn't seen one Asian individual yet. This is odd considering that China bought the fishing rights off the coast of Sierra Leone. As you cross into the Atlantic, all the fishing vessels flying the flag of China become prevalent. Apparently, they don't get to shore often.

We left Family Kingdom and headed to the restaurant, and by "we" I mean Lee, Solomon, Richard, Brother Arnold, and myself. It was located on the main road down a steep driveway. It was a place called Indochine.

The interior was very clean, and the staff was friendly. I was informed that the owner was from Vietnam. We sat down, and I picked up a menu not sure what to expect. To my surprise, it looked like a menu you might find in America.

After two weeks of being in Africa, you would have thought that I'd have had the currency figured out, but no! Not me! Money was getting low, and I had to watch what I ordered. During my trip, I was told that I couldn't use credit cards in most places. So, I had to use cash. I ended up looking for something I recognized that would be fairly cheap. But much to my surprise, when the food came, it was outstanding.

Someone in our group ordered sweet and sour chicken, and to date, that was the best I have ever tasted anywhere. When my food arrived, it, too, was outstanding. We had a wonderful meal with a sweet time of fellowship.

When people ask me about Chinese restaurants, I tell them the two best places that this Kearny boy ever had were in Waycross, GA and Freetown, Sierra Leone. If you are ever in Freetown, on Aberdeen Road, look for gates and a steep curvy driveway. Once you find it, get yourself a good meal at

Indochine. Tell them Matt Swiatkowski sent you. I should mention that telling them I sent you probably won't help you, and they won't know or remember me; however, it may make you sound important.

"T" For Texas

Sunday

Solomon came to our rooms the next morning to gather us only to discover that Brother Arnold was not feeling well. Brother Arnold decided he would stay at the hotel and rest.

We had our two eggs and other items for breakfast, and then, we made our way into Freetown to a section that was called Texas. I was told it was a very rough part of town and had a reputation for drugs, witchcraft, Satanism, and many other vices.

The church we would be going to was a new church and was still small. As we made our way to the church, I noticed that the one thing you never quite got over was the extent of the poverty.

There was a small creek that ran through one part of the area. It had raw sewage in it as well as garbage. I was even more shocked and saddened to see children playing in the water and some washing clothes.

I was prepared to preach when we reached the church, but I wasn't sure if I would or not. Solomon told me that he wasn't sure either. He said that the pastor may or may not let me, so I would leave it in the Lord's hands. I am not the type of man who walks up and asks to preach in another man's church.

The church was on a large front porch and had a small but good size crowd in attendance. We sang from a hymnal, but there were very few of them. The few that they did have were pretty worn out, but we sang anyway. The preacher introduced us and then proceeded to preach.

I can't blame the man. After all, as a pastor, you study and prepare before preaching. So if a stranger walks up, you're not just going to let him preach. I know I wouldn't!

I was glad to be there. I enjoyed the service and my time with the people. After the message, the preacher asked me to come up, introduce myself, and say something. I wasn't sure what that meant, so while he was talking, I asked Solomon what to do.

"Tell them about yourself and preach," he said.

"But is he asking me to preach or just say hello?" I asked.

"Say hello and preach," he replied.

So with that, I went up, said hello, introduced myself, and preached. There was a sweet spirit as I spoke, so I did not preach long. I also did not need an interpreter. The people all shook my hand and thanked me afterwards. They expressed a need for more hymnals and even a keyboard. I promised that I would send them the hymnals and even a keyboard. It might take a while, but they would receive them.

I asked if we could get a group photo, and they all agreed. We went out in front of the church and took a picture. I assumed that it was the end of everything, and Solomon thought so, too. We then left after saying our goodbyes, but what they failed to tell us was that they were making a gift for me. Some dear saint was in a back room sewing a nice shirt. Solomon was able to secure this for me before we left Sierra Leone, and I keep it as a cherished memory of these dear people.

When I returned home, we raised money for the items, bought the hymnals, and bought a good keyboard. We sent them to Brother Arnold who, soon afterwards, had them placed in a container, and then, off they went.

Fire In the Water

There aren't really any Sunday evening church services in Sierra Leone for many reasons. So, that night, we had a meeting with local pastors to talk and deal with some of their concerns. It was a productive meeting, and all went well.

Afterwards, we went to a restaurant called the Lighthouse. It wasn't far from our hotel. In fact, it was right next to it, but a little inlet of water separated us. In order to reach the restaurant, we had to drive up the hill and around. It was technically a hotel with a fancy restaurant. We sat out on an open patio over the water and had a wonderful time.

We looked out over the ocean and saw a man with a long wooden stick going into the water from the shoreline. He made his way through the water and came close to where we were sitting. He then proceeded to set the two ends of the stick on fire and began to twirl and toss it into the air. He was super talented, and I thought I would definitely end up setting myself on fire had I tried it. He was looking for a little money, and so, Brother Arnold went over to the edge of the balcony and tossed him a few dollars.

Chapter Thirteen

HEADING HOME

MONDAY

I'm Going to Kill Those Little Brats

I woke up excited and saddened that we would be leaving by the end of the day. Once again, we ate breakfast at family kingdom and then went over to the beach for one last look.

Earlier that morning, Lee said he was going for a swim but was complaining that the day before his sandals had been stolen off the beach. When we arrived at the beach, I saw his sandals and towel. He had taken a stick and placed it through the weave and into the sand. I really don't know what he thought this was going to do, but I decided to have some fun. I quickly removed the stick, took his sandals, and placed them under a nearby log. A man on the beach saw me do this, and I motioned with my finger to my lips to be quiet and smiled.

We walked around and saw Lee coming out of the water. He was lightly smiling and chatting, but his countenance changed when he saw his sandals missing. His face quickly darkened in anger, and he said, "If I catch that little brat, I'll kill 'em."

He started looking around to see if anybody nearby had his sandals. We all started laughing. He thought we were laughing at him and muttered under his breath. Then, we went and pulled his shoes out from under the log. The man who I told to keep the secret was rolling on the beach laughing. Even

Lee had to laugh at the joke and threatened revenge, but then said God had already punished me by not letting me have my clothes for two weeks.

On the beach near the road were merchants selling wood carvings, and I wanted to buy some souvenirs for my family. I knew there would be a white man markup price. So I went over and looked around. They all began to try to bargain with me with incredibly high prices. I told them I was just looking and admiring their work. I then went back and told Solomon what I wanted. He waited and then went over to buy the items I had explained to him. They knew what he was doing. There was a lot of yelling and screaming, but in the end, he bought the items at a fair price.

Water Taxi Please and Don't Spare the Engine

The time had come to leave, and I thought we would take the broken-down ferry again, but I was informed that we were going in style and would have some fun.

"How?" I asked.

I was then told about the water taxi. It was a small boat with two large motors built for speed that carried passengers across the river. We would go flying across the water and arrive at Pelican Terminal, a dock at Lungi where the airport was.

I was excited about the boat ride. We all got on board with great anticipation. We started out slowly, but as soon as we moved away from the dock area they opened up the two motors, and we began to move. . . for a minute or two anyway. Then we slowed down but kept moving slowly.

I had positioned myself near the back of the boat while Lee, Richard, Solomon (who was going for the ride), and Brother Arnold all sat up front. One of the employees walked to the back and started working on one of the engines. There was yelling and talking going on between the workmen, but eventually, we were told that the engine was broken. We only had one left and would have to limp across the water.

"Just great," I thought to myself.

My comrades all turned around, looked at me, and started calling me Jonah. They threatened to throw me overboard. After all, if something could go wrong on this trip, it seemed that it would, and I was somehow connected to it. I laughed at their Jonah jokes, but if they took one step towards me, I was going to go full blown Chuck Norris or Barney Fife. We slowly made our way across, but I think the ferry we were on the first night might have been faster.

Hurry Up and Sweat

The airport required us to arrive a full three hours before our flight. So, once we were at the airport, we said goodbye to Solomon. This was bittersweet as I had grown to love this dear man and counted him as a brother.

We made our way through security, customs, and all kinds of good stuff. Once we left that section of the airport, we made our way into a large open area where everyone stood and waited. It was basically a large hanger but decorated a little better. To top it all off, there was no air conditioning at all. It was brutally hot, and we were all soaking wet with perspiration.

A man I recognized from the Brussels office in Freetown approached me all excited and told me to follow him. I did as he said, but I was nervous as to what was happening. The last thing I wanted was to be in a foreign country and have customs pull me out and take me away.

"What is this for?" I asked.

"Follow me!" was his only response.

My compatriots all laughed and waved as I walked off. He assured me I would not miss my flight, and we went into an office. There were several people present in the room. They all looked solemn and stared at me as I entered. The office was air conditioned, and it felt good. I figured if they were to beat me or lock me up, at least I wouldn't be sweating.

"Mr. Swiatkowski, we have good news! We have your luggage, and it is in Brussels," a man (who I had never laid eyes on before) said.

I was a little shocked at his "news" because I already knew this.

"Yes, I know. Someone called me Saturday and informed me of this," I told them.

They looked surprised and began to yell at each other in a language I did not understand. They apologized for any inconvenience, and I assured them that it was all good, I did quite well, and appreciated their gift of 100 dollars. Again, I did not want to be angry or do anything that would ruin my Christian testimony. These people had done nothing wrong and were very kind; they did not deserve any angry talk from me. They were friendly, and I was kind as well.

I reluctantly left the office. If I had just one more nerve, I would have asked for a first-class upgrade for my troubles.

But I didn't.

I made my way back to my friends who were all very serious and wanting to know what had happened. I tried to think of a good story to tell them like they were looking for drugs or something crazy, but my brain was too fried from the heat. So, I simply told them the truth.

Close the Curtains on the Schlubs

We stood there for a little while longer and finally began the boarding process for the plane. We made our way on board, and I found that my seat was right behind first class. I was drenched with sweat, the people around me were the same, and I believe the guy next to me had a goat under his jacket . . . or at least it smelled that way. I sat there looking into first class and admiring the luxurious seats.

Sitting for long periods of time was extremely painful for me. In two years, my right hip will have to be replaced because all the cartilage will be gone, and it will be bone on bone. Right now, I am limping on a daily basis and struggle with the basics.

As I sat there, I noticed a stewardess with a large, metal tray carrying small, cold, moist towels. She was using tongs to grab them and distribute them to the people in first class. I sat there looking, with my mouth open, and imagining what they felt like. How nice it would be just to wipe my face and neck down with that little baby.

She looked over, saw me, gave me a nice smile, and made her way towards me. My eyes grew big as she approached. The whole time she walked towards me, she was looking and smiling at me.

By the time she reached me, I was wearing a smile. She reached up, and I begin to rise out of my seat with cool anticipation. I couldn't help thinking that maybe I would get one of those cool towels. After all, we were all one giant sweat ball. But then, with her free hand, she grabbed the curtain that separated first class from the minions in steerage, and she forcefully closed it.

I never saw her again.

Just like that I was lifted up only to be dashed onto the rocks. It reminded me of my dating life before I met my wife.

As the plane departed, I looked one more time out the window and waved goodbye to that dear country.

TAKE NOTE SWIATKOWSKI

"But a certain Samaritan, as he journeyed, came where he was: and when he saw him, he had compassion on him. And went to him, and bound up his wounds, pouring in oil and wine, and set him on his own beast, and brought him to an inn, and took care of him. And on the morrow when he departed, he took out two pence, and gave them to the host, and said unto him, 'Take care of him; and whatsoever thou spendest more, when I come again, I will repay thee.'" (Luke 10:33-35).

The parable of the Good Samaritan is a famous one, and its truths will never perish. How much does it cost to be kind to someone? How much effort can it take? I realize that there are people who add up the cost for all things with businesses, and the bottom line is always going to be the bottom line. How much would it cost an airline to hand out cold, damp towels to all its passengers who have been standing in a

100-degree hangar for several hours? I don't know, but I do know it would have been kind of them to do so.

Now, my message is not to corporations but to Christians. How much does it cost us to be kind to people on an hourly basis? Let the guy merge who is trying to hop onto the highway, hold a door, say thank you, or relinquish a seat.

I came upon a traffic jam one day, apparently, a young lady had broken down. I was working, and I mumbled under my breath as I went around her. After all, I was on the clock, and there was work to be done. No sooner had I gone around her then the Spirit of God smote my heart and asked why I hadn't helped her.

"Well, Lord, I'm a plumber not a mechanic," I replied knowing full well that it was just a poor excuse.

His only response was telling me go back and help her. I swung a U turn and headed back. I was praying she was still there, because if she wasn't, I was afraid of what the Lord would do to me.

There she was, just sitting in her car crying. Now, may I remind you that this was before cell phones; however, even if she had one and called for help, it is still unnerving sitting there, blocking traffic while people curse at you and yell. Did it ever occur to you, when you see someone broken down, that they didn't plan that to happen? That they didn't wake up and say, "I hope my car breaks down and ruins people's day"?

I approached the car and asked if help was on the way. She rolled her window down halfway and said no.

Did I mention it was raining?

Well, it was.

I told her that I would push the car to a parking lot on the other side of the intersection. I instructed her to put the car in neutral and to not hit the brake. I saw that people were watching us, but again, no one offered to help us.

The light changed, and I was able to push the car to the lot where there was a pay phone. I gave her a Gospel tract and was on my way. Altogether, it took about 15 minutes of my day and cost me nothing. Sometimes, kindness does cost money, like in the case of the parable we mentioned, but that's not why we do it. We do it for the Lord, and because it's the right thing to do.

TUESDAY

Together Again

We flew through the night and landed in Brussels at 6:30 am. Once there, I immediately proceeded to the lost and found. I presented my information, they handed me my bag, and I was on my way.

I found a bench and opened my suitcase only to find that it had been pilfered. My electric Braun razor that was a Father's Day gift was gone, the Mets and Yankee baseball hats that were for the preachers in Africa were gone, and a canvas sun hat (the kind with the brim all the way around it) was gone.

"Who would want that?" I thought.

I had worn it for a few years, so the band inside was stained with my sweat. With that being the case, some individual must have been desperate. I was aggravated that a worker would be low enough to steal another man's property.

At 7:15 am, I had to check my bag back in and go through security to get to the terminal. I asked where the United terminal for bag checking was, and they told me what number to go to.

At this point, I reached another dilemma. The gate number I was given did not exist. So, I asked again and was told the same number. Frustrated, I walked around to double check all the numbers. Once again, it did not exist. So, I asked one more time. There was a new person at the desk, and they informed me that the number was correct; however, United would come place a temporary podium up with posts and retractable barriers soon. They showed me where they would do this.

I was thankful for their kindness.

I stood at the spot indicated and waited. They said that the plane would be arriving at 8:00 am. It was now 7:25 am. I decided to stand and wait so that I'd be the first in line. I was afraid that if I left, I would return to a long line and be there until who knows when. Sure enough, workers came and started setting things up.

"It's still going to be a few minutes before everything is ready," the lady who worked there told me.

"That's fine. I don't mind waiting. Just take your time," I said.

Then they set everything up so that there were two lines. Now, keep in mind that I had been there since 7:25, and it was now 8:15. Some guy came along and stood in the second line they established.

I found myself thinking, *"There is no way this guy is going before me! I'll take him out before that happens! I have been waiting longer than he has, and I am only out here because someone lost my luggage."*

We both kind of looked at each other with that game on face, but he was older, so I knew I could take him down if I had to.

I was tired, aggravated, had a thin salty crust of dried sweat all over me, and needed to brush my teeth. In reality, while these thoughts ran through my head, I knew it would all work out.

I just wanted to be first.

When they were ready to open, a lady cut in front of everyone, walked up to the podium, and started asking questions. By then there was a long line of people in both lines. The mumbling began behind me, and to make matters worse, the United workers were helping her and answering her questions.

I could hear people saying in low voices, "Get in line and wait," "I don't believe this," and other phrases that will go unmentioned.

Finally, the worker looked up and asked for the next person. The man next to me jumped forward. Before I could say or do anything, the worker told him to wait because I had been there longer, so she would help me first.

Praise God, someone cared!

I told my bag I loved it, gave it a slight hug, and waved goodbye one last time.

TAKE NOTE SWIATKOWSKI

The word "stuff" describes "matter or thing; particularly, that which is trifling or worthless; a very extensive use of the word. Flattery is fulsome stuff; poor poetry is miserable stuff" ("Stuff").

It's amazing how we worry over "stuff." This word is found some 16 times in scripture, and when it's used, it is usually not in a flattering way.

"Also regard not your stuff; for the good of all the land of Egypt is yours" (Genesis 45:20).

"Therefore they enquired of the LORD further, if the man should yet come thither. And the LORD answered, Behold, he hath hid himself among the stuff" (I Samuel 10:22).

All of our effort, strain, and anxiety over "stuff," not even expensive "stuff," is so trivial. If I added up the cost of the contents that were thrown in the suitcase (which I purchased in 1988 when I went to college) it would probably all be worth about $600.00. Everything that was missing could easily be replaced. Everything I had packed would eventually wear out, be thrown out, and one day, replaced.

There I was, going home that day and still stressing about my "stuff." While we should be careful with our "stuff," we must never let the love of it control us. Occasionally on the trip, I let my "stuff" get to me.

Back to the USA

We boarded our plane at noon and would arrive in Dulles at 2:20 pm. This was because of the time difference. It would be a long eight-hour flight. I sat next to Brother Arnold, and we had a pleasant time talking and mingling on the plane.

Eventually, the captain announced that we would be landing and gave us the weather update. It was sunny and 38 degrees. This was going to be cold compared to the weather we had just been in for the last two weeks, but it was home. The plane approached and when the wheels hit the ground, I broke out in a cheer and applause as did half the plane.

I made it through customs. All the while I had a stupid smile on my face because I was about to see my dear wife, kids, and my church family. However, my smile quickly disappeared when I was informed that my flight to Newark was canceled.

I just stood there with no smile, but still a stupid look on my face. My jaw was sitting on my chest as I looked on in disbelief. Here it came. . . that low rumbling within my flesh. I was about to lose it on some dear worker who had no control over this problem when my companions all began laughing.

"No. It can't be. He has suffered enough!" they all said through their laughter.

I looked at the worker standing before me.

"WHAT?! How can it be cancelled?!" I asked in shock.

"It looks like there were not enough people for the flight, so it was cancelled. However, there's another flight leaving in a few minutes, and we could get you on that one for no extra charge."

"I'll take it! Where is it?" I immediately said.

"Hold on. . . it's too far to walk."

He made a phone call and put me on one of those golf carts where you sit facing backwards. I quickly said goodbye to my friends, and I was off. I really wished I had more time to say goodbye, but the plane was leaving very soon.

I don't really like the golf carts at the airport. As you pass people, you stare at them, and they stare at you. It was apparent that they are wondering what was wrong with me, the lazy guy who couldn't walk, but I didn't care. We zipped through the crowds, honked the weak, little horn, and then I was at my terminal with the flight ready to go.

My plan was that (after we got into the airport) I would have time to find a restroom and freshen up. I needed to brush my teeth, change my shirt, and apply fresh deodorant, but the flight change did not allow any of that. So I boarded the flight as I was.

It was a very small jet plane, and there were only a handful of people on it. I found my seat next to a young man. I was feeling very self-conscious because I had sat next to stinky people before, and I did not want to be one of them. I tried to sneak a whiff of myself to see if I did stink or if it was just me being oversensitive. I even tried to smell my breath, but I think you have to have a super case of halitosis to smell your own bad breath. Either way, I was not comfortable sitting so close to this fella.

Once we were ready to take off, I noticed that there was plenty of room and vacant seats on the plane, so I asked the stewardess if I could sit where I wanted. She told me to help myself. I politely excused myself from the young man next to me and found an empty row. If I did stink from my long journey, at least I would do so in my own row and not bother anyone else.

You Have Got to Be Kidding Me

The flight was short, in under an hour, I was back home. I made my way to the baggage carousel (or what I call the luggage dispenser) and waited. . . and waited. . . and waited just a little more. I asked an airport attendee if they were done with the luggage from my flight, and they said that they were.

I had no luggage. . . again.

I made my way to the lost and found where they did a quick search to assure me that my luggage was not in Newark. They told me they would find it and deliver it to me. All I had to do was fill out a slip describing my luggage.

I wanted to write that my suitcase was half empty because people had stolen my stuff. Then I thought about mentioning that most of the contents that remained in my luggage were all clean because it had never been worn on my trip . . . but I didn't. I was in a good mood because I was glad to be home.

It's like the old song says, "be it ever so humble, there's no place like home." To the Africans, I was a rich man. I told them that I was not a financially rich person, but even so, I looked forward to being home in my modest surroundings. I missed my wife, children, my own bed, and my own pillow.

As a quick side note, if you want a good vacation, try to take your own pillow along. I promise you, it will make all the difference.

I was looking forward to my refrigerator filled with food that I could eat whenever I wanted. I was craving a good pizza and a good old-fashioned, American hamburger. Just the thought of them both got my mouth watering. And of course, a steak. Oh, how I longed for a good, thick, juicy steak cooked medium. I missed my hometown and friends. Just to go and sit in my recliner at home and use paved roads on the way there sounded like a dream come true. And water, cold water (not from a bottle that was the same temperature as the air), that sounded like paradise.

Listening to the way I was talking, you'd think I had been away for years. You'd think that I was ungrateful, but nothing could be further from the truth. I loved Africa and the people. I loved how they gave me the best they had. They watched over me, cared for me, and loved me. I was, and always will be, humbled by the kindness of my friends there. There are many things I missed about Africa: its beautiful scenery, the warm ocean, the jungle, and villages scattered throughout the country. Even the food was unique and a blessing. But again, most of all, I missed those dear people.

I tried using my Verizon phone to call home, but it wouldn't work. It didn't work in Africa or Europe either. So, there I was, sitting in America (right next to a Verizon sign), and still, I couldn't make a phone call. I took out a little piece of paper I had with all the instructions, the different numbers to dial, along with all of the prompts. . . but nothing.

I learned a very important lesson that day: never call Verizon to tell them you're leaving the country because they will mail and charge you for a phone that's pretty much useless all around the world.

I ended up looking for a payphone so I could call home.

While I sat in the airport (before making my call to home) it was a time of reflection for me. I wanted to call home, but I found myself unable to do anything except sit and think. I was only fifteen minutes from my house. I had been on a trip that took me to the other side of the world. I had seen things I never dreamed I would ever see. I had made new friends and preached to thousands. I had seen true poverty and what it was like, and I saw true happiness. Those that were happy were not so because they had possessions, but instead they were happy because they had Christ.

I was still in a bit of shock. I had actually gone to Africa. . . me. . . a boy from Kearny. I was stunned, and all I could do was sit there deep in thought and in prayer as I thanked my Father for all He had done for me.

Hundreds of people were passing by me while I sat there in the airport, but to be honest, I was oblivious to them all. A smile came to my face as I thought about my adventure and mishaps. It was there that I thought I should take all of my diary entries and make them into a book.

"Me. . . write a book? That won't happen," I thought to myself.

Time went fast, but I eventually realized I had been sitting there for too long. I needed to call home. I wanted so desperately to see my wife and kids.

I had to reverse the charges because I had no change for my phone call. I could have bought something to get change, but I didn't want to waste any more time. Fighting with my Verizon phone had wasted enough of my time already. Renee accepted the charges on the phone call, and I was glad.

"Where are you?" she asked.

"I'm at the Newark airport. When do you think you could get here to pick me up?" I replied.

"I'll be there right away!" she responded excitedly.

We arranged a pick-up location because, again, she could not call me when she arrived at the airport since I had a Verizon phone that wouldn't work.

I stood there waiting.

I was so glad to see our van coming around the bend a short time later with my wife looking for me. She pulled up but could not get out and hug me because of our pick-up area. So, I hopped in, reached over and kissed my wife, and then said hello to my kids. It was Melanie, Ethan, and Evan. Matthew was away at college, so I would call and talk to him later.

The kids all asked how the trip was, what happened, and all kinds of questions. Renee had a smile on her face that lit up the car as she drove us back home. She didn't talk much as her attention was focused on navigating us out of the airport. Newark airport can be interesting to try and find your way out of. Getting in is easy, but they make you pay to leave.

Once home in our driveway, we all hopped out of the van and hugged and kissed. To anyone watching it would have seemed like I had been gone for years. Renee hadn't been sure when I was going to get home, but she had prepared a delicious home cooked meal. When we were first married, she would ask me what food I liked so she could buy it and prepare meals.

"Sweetheart, let me give you a list of what I don't like," I told her.

The list was really short.

She prepared a Pot Roast with potatoes, carrots, and completed it with homemade gravy and rye bread. We ate and talked all about my trip, and they told me all that had happened while I was away.

It was a magical moment.

Years earlier, I had read a letter a Civil War soldier wrote after he returned home. He said the feeling he had was strange. While working in the corn fields, it seemed like he had never left home at all, but on the other hand, it seemed he had been gone forever. This is exactly how I was feeling, and it would take some time to adjust back to my normal routine.

That night, the moment my body hit the bed I crashed into a very deep, coma-like sleep. All those who have traveled across time zones know that it takes a few days to adjust to a normal schedule.

WEDNESDAY

We went to church that Wednesday evening, and everyone gave me a hero's welcome home. They had heard from Renee about my missing luggage and plane cancelations. Everyone wanted to hear the stories of Africa and what it was like. We had a great time, and everyone had a good laugh at my misadventures.

We arrived home from service, and I was exhausted as I was still suffering from jet lag. No sooner had we walked in the door than I received a phone call. It was United Airlines, and they would be delivering my luggage shortly.

Sure enough, the man arrived and handed it off to me. Before he did, he asked me if it was mine. I looked at it carefully and told him that it was. Then he left. That was it.

I made a quick inspection of my bag and found that nothing else was stolen. Thankfully, not all of the good stuff had been taken. I put it down and decided that I would unpack it the next day. I was tired and needed a good night's rest.

My luggage had seen the world and so had I. I could only hope that it was blessed as much as I was.

Chapter Fourteen

THE CONCLUSION

As a small boy, I would go to Sunday school with my three brothers: Eddie, Chester, and Steven along with my older sister, Susie. Later, my younger sister, Nancy, would attend. I have fond memories of us all leaving the house and walking up the hill to church. Door to door, it was probably only one hundred and fifty yards. I remember how happy it would make me to go to church with my siblings, all of us with our Bibles walking up the hill, talking and laughing, and sometimes even arguing.

I always enjoyed being around my siblings. I loved them dearly, and I knew they loved me. The first time they took me to church, I was very young. My mom said a little while after we had left there was a knock at the door. When she answered it, our pastor, Pastor Chris, stood there holding me as I was crying. He said, with a warm smile, "He misses his mommy. Give him some time and let him come back."

He was a kind man.

Later, as my brothers got older, they began to rebel and refused to go to Sunday school. Eddie was the first, then later Chet, and then Steve. I would get dressed, they all would be sleeping, and I would ask if they wanted to go. It made me sad and even angry when they refused because I knew it was hurting my mom when they would act in such a manner.

When they refused, it was just my two sisters and me that would walk up the hill. Just as there is a first time for something, like when all six of us made the walk up the hill, there is always a last time. That day is only known to the

Lord, and He knows when the last time was when we all sat in Sunday school together. I think of the times when we were all there. If I'm honest, I often wish for those days again, but I know it is not possible.

My mom, dad, and three brothers are all home with the Lord now. They will have to wait for me to finish my course along with Susie and Nancy. One day, we can all meet at the feet of the Lord. Heaven is a wonderful place, my friend.

While in Sunday school, we would go over Bible verses for memorization. Now, I can't be sure which was the first verse I ever memorized. It's probably a toss-up between Isaiah 53:6, "All we like sheep have gone astray; we have turned every one to his own way; and the LORD hath laid on him the iniquity of us all." And Proverbs 3:5-6, "Trust in the LORD with all thine heart; and lean not unto thine own understanding. In all thy ways acknowledge him, and he shall direct thy paths."

No matter which one it was, they are both forever in mind and can be quoted without flaw. I am indebted to my pastor and teachers for helping me memorize the word of God. There were other verses that were memorized as well, and again, they can be quoted.

It's true that Isaiah 53:6 tells you how to obtain eternal life. We obtain it through the finished work of Christ. I read a story once that said the evangelist R.A. Torrey was rushing to catch a train when a man came alongside him and asked how he could be saved. The train was slowly pulling away from the station, and as Dr. Torrey jumped on the train, he told the man go to Isaiah 53:6. He told him to go in at the first "All" and come out at the last "All," and he'd be saved.

All of us are like sheep that are following our own desires and will. We are doing what pleases us with little regard to the damage we are doing to those around us. Man has a serious sin problem, and there is no earthly remedy for it. But the verse continues to tell us that God placed the sins of the world upon the Lord, Jesus Christ. He paid the sin debt for ALL mankind. Not just a select few, but all men. There is no other sacrifice, there is no other remedy.

Proverbs 3:5-6 will teach you how to live a Christian life.

Growing up, we also had pictures on the walls with Bible verses in them. I found that, when my mind would drift, I would read the signs. Little did I realize then that scripture was being placed into my heart. Now that I am a pastor, I understand the necessity of all this. Scripture teaches us that, "Thy word have I hid in mine heart, that I might not sin against thee" (Psalm 119:11). It also tells us in Romans 14:23 ". . .for whatsoever is not of faith is sin." Clearly put, when we have a lack of faith, we are sinning.

I tell you all of this to reach the point I want to make. Proverbs 3:5-6 has become my life's verse. To me, it is so powerful and covers all the bases. If I am asked to preach somewhere, young people have asked me to sign their Bibles. Apparently, it's a popular thing to do, but I always feel funny doing it. I am not a big shot, nor do I think highly of myself, but I do it. I always write the book chapter and verse Proverbs 3:5-6.

This verse was being taught to me in Africa, and I didn't even realize it.

First: Trust In the Lord with All Thine Heart

The truth found in Proverbs 3:5-6 is emphasized throughout all of scripture. We see that Adam and Eve failed to apply its truth and fell into sin. Abraham failed to trust when the famine hit and then ran to Egypt. Isaac lied about his wife. Jacob failed to trust the Lord and bought property in Shechem when he should have been in Bethel. Moses failed when he struck the rock the second time instead of speaking to it as the Lord commanded. King Saul lost his kingdom when he offered sacrifice without Samuel and refused to obey all of God's commands concerning the Amalekites. On and on the list goes in the Bible, and often, there is heartache involved when this verse is not applied. The scripture says that these things are an example for us to learn from. The sad truth is, we don't learn from them. When we fail to learn from Biblical example, we are forced by the Lord to learn them through our own trials.

I learned some valuable lessons from the Lord that I needed while on my trip. I have shared and detailed them all in the previous chapters. It all began when there was a major storm that disrupted the entire Northeast corridor. Airlines and trains were all off schedule and canceled. I did not know how much the storm had affected everything until I was at the airport. It was then that I needed the Lord to help me, and He helped me every single step of the way. I saw Him do great things for me. He moved the hearts of people, held airplanes still, provided for me, and so much more. I had to trust Him because no one else could help me.

When we know the Lord, we must never forget that He has promised to never leave us. His Holy Spirit is sealed within us until the Day of Redemption (Ephesian 4:30). If that truth is firmly fixed in our hearts, then why do we have such a difficult time trusting Him?

I can trust God to do the right thing for me. He is not against me, but for me. He will guide me to green pastures, beside still waters, and He will be with me when I am in the valley of the shadow of death. He is my comforter and guide into all truth. He will not hurt me. Too often, we put our faith in people and have our hearts broken. Even so, we continue to have faith and put our trust in people. I find it interesting that we fail to have that same spirit of faith when it comes to walking with our Saviour.

Abraham learned to trust the Lord even though He asked for the life of his son Isaac. Joshua trusted Him when he marched around Jericho. Gideon confided in Him when his army was reduced to 300 men. Esther stepped out in faith and stood before her husband at a time when it could have cost her, her life. She uttered, "If I perish, I perish."

She knew who was in control. Examples such as these go on throughout all of scripture.

I can personally say that it's easy to trust God when you have resources around you to help you out if you feel God is not stepping in. However, to be in a situation or place in life where you are constantly in need, well that is another thing completely.

I learned by watching the people of Sierra Leone and Liberia that we need God all the time. I watched how they trusted Him, and I was convicted and humbled by their child-like faith. I saw how God helped them even through the atrocities.

Second: Lean Not Onto Your Own Understanding

Whatever you're thinking, you often must do the opposite. Scripture is filled with many of these great paradoxes.

If you want to receive, you must learn to give.

> "I have showed you all things, how that so labouring ye ought to support the weak, and to remember the words of the Lord Jesus, how he said, It is more blessed to give than to receive" (Acts 20:35).

If you want to be exalted, you must go down.

> "Humble yourselves in the sight of the Lord, and he shall lift you up" (James 4:10).

If you want strength, you must be weak.

> "Therefore I take pleasure in infirmities, in reproaches, in necessities, in persecutions, in distresses for Christ's sake: for when I am weak, then am I strong" (II Corinthians 12:10).

If you want freedom, be a servant.

> "Being then made free from sin, ye became the servants of righteousness" (Romans 6:18).

If you want life, you have to die.

> "Verily, verily, I say unto you, Except a corn of wheat fall into the ground and die, it abideth alone: but if it die, it bringeth forth much fruit. He that loveth his life shall lose it; and he that hateth his life in this world shall keep it unto life eternal" (John 12:24-25).

With these scriptural truths in place, we are reminded of Proverbs 3:5-6, "lean not on your own understanding."

You may be wondering how this applied while on my trip. Well, it's simple. I learned that I did not need all the small things I thought I needed.

All of my sermons and handouts were in my suitcase. I did not have them when I preached. All I had was my Bible, the Holy Spirit, my salvation in Christ, and a blessed Father who loved me and cared for me. What more did I need?

I read, many years ago, that famed missionary and explorer, David Livingstone, landed in Africa with trunk loads of books and possessions. The further he went on his journey, the more things he dropped off until one day, he only had his minor possessions and his Bible. When I read his story, I thought it was the most amazing thing. On my trip to Africa, I found it to be true.

Many a godly person may discover that, if they let the Lord help them, they don't need as much as they think they need. There is nothing wrong with a good library of books, but never neglect the book that all the others are writing about.

Our human wisdom teaches that we need much if we want to accomplish something. However, according to the Bible, a donkey's jawbone in the hand of Samson was enough to take care of a thousand Philistines, and a rod in the hand of Moses was enough to shake Egypt to its foundations. God provides everything that we need to further His kingdom.

It is important that we learn to trust God and lean upon His word. We need to let our hearts rest in His wisdom and not in an individual (no matter how godly they may seem).

When it comes to service to God, many feel inadequate, but if we surrender to him, keep our noses in scripture, and stay dependent upon the Holy Spirit, it will be enough. I can say this from my own, personal experience.

Materialism has always been one of the greatest hindrances to a personal relationship with the Lord. If we are materialistic then, most likely, we don't have any thoughts of sacrificing or offering anything for our Lord and Saviour, Jesus Christ. After receiving Christ as Saviour, we need to accept the fact that we are to live a life of service and sacrifice for Him. Only then can we be truly satisfied.

Don't lean on personal wisdom if it contradicts the Word of God.

Third: but in thy ways, acknowledge Him

What does it mean to acknowledge God? I have noticed that most people will often act differently depending on where they are and who they are with.

One night, I was out visiting and looking for a lady who had come to our church. There was some confusion as to her address. I found the house that I thought was hers, walked up the pathway to her house, and just as I was about to knock on the front door, I heard the couple in the house start screaming and yelling at each other. I stood there in shock and listened to the awful things they were saying to each other. I wondered if I should knock on the door or not. I prayed and felt like the Lord was leading me to knock, so I did. The husband answered the door. He was very calm and pleasant.

"Is this the same guy who was screaming a minute ago?" I thought to myself.

I explained who I was, and who I was looking for. He turned to his wife and said, "Sweetheart, there is a pastor here, and he is looking for so and so; do you know her?"

"No, honey. I don't think so," she replied

They were using loving and sweet tones.

I thought to myself, *"Hey buddy, you weren't calling her sweetheart a few seconds ago! And lady, you weren't calling him honey!"*

I handed them both a gospel tract and invited them to church. Once again, they very sweetly responded that they would think about it. We said goodbye, the door was closed, and WWIII immediately broke out inside the house.

They, like so many others, wear one face in one situation and another face for another. That is not the child of God's mindset or attitude.

To make proper application of this verse, we must understand that it doesn't mean to simply acknowledge His presence. It is so much more. It means that, as Christians, we are to act like Christ in all that we do no matter what circumstances we are in. Every aspect of our life should reflect Christ. Everything we do should show the character of Christ. Our work ethic, how we vote, and the decisions that we make each day should show who God is. Our choices and actions should not be based upon our will or our gut feelings. After prayer and spending time in the Word, we should then act according to Biblical/Godly principles.

In the book of Acts, how did Steven react when he was being stoned by a crowd? Well, he acted Christ-like. He acknowledged the Lord in his life. When Paul and Silas were in jail in Philippi, they were beaten and chained. How did they respond? They acted like Christ. They prayed and sang, but what they were actually doing through their actions was acknowledging Christ. Their mindset and actions led to the conversion of the Philippian jailer and his family.

Just think, if they acted like many "Christians" today, they would have been screaming and threatening lawsuits. . . along with getting mad at God. We often wonder why we have so few conversions in today's generation. Maybe it's because we see so little of Christ in His so-called disciples. When the Apostle Paul led a thief and runaway slave named Onesimus to Christ, he told him to go back to his master, and he instructed Philemon, the master, to treat him as a brother in Christ. In other words, both parties were to acknowledge the Lord in the situation.

While in Africa, there were quite a few moments of frustration. It would have been easy to scream and treat the people around me poorly, but if I did that, I would not have been acknowledging the Lord. I would have turned people away from God and would have been a lousy representative of my Lord and Saviour. Every time I began to feel frustrated and wanted to vent, the Holy Spirit reminded me of who I was and how I was to act.

Proverbs 3:5-6 was placed in my heart as a small boy. It helped prevent me from sinning. Isn't that why we memorize scripture, so we will not sin against the Lord? To acknowledge God means to submit everything to Him in our lives. In other words, surrender your will to His and allow yourself to be a servant to Christ. We call Him master, but is He our master?

Fourth: He Shall Direct Thy Path

The last part of Proverbs 3:5-6 ends with a promise. It says that He will direct our path. Sadly, too many people neglect the first part of this verse, but they think this phrase will apply to their lives.

This part is conditional.

It hinges on what has already been said. Friend, God is not going to direct your path if you do not put Him first and obey Him.

There is an order to things, and too often, people fail to realize that. They want to skip all that's necessary or required and still receive the benefits at the end; However, God doesn't work that way. In my life, I learned many lessons, but those lessons need to be put into action if you want God's blessing. We cannot ignore the Lord and expect Him to move and work on our behalf. Too often, that's how most parents operate.

I was in Maryland at a rest stop on I-95. My son and I were eating a meal at a picnic bench. A table away from us there was a mom and her five-year-old daughter. The entire time they were there, the mother kept telling her daughter over, and over, and over, and over to eat her chicken nuggets or she wouldn't get ice cream. I whispered to my son to mark it down, that kid would get ice cream.

"But Dad, she isn't eating the nuggets!" he protested.

"Trust me, if we were gamblers (which we're not), we would bet the ranch and grandma that that little girl," I jerked my thumb in her direction, "is getting ice cream," I said.

We watched them get up and leave (the nuggets still on the table). We also left to go get a few things done. About ten minutes later, I noticed the mom walking out the door to the parking lot holding her daughter's hand. There was the girl, licking an ice cream cone.

"Dad, how did you know?" my son asked.

"Experience with humans, son," was my response.

Sadly, that's how we think God is. We think that we can go through life ignoring all of His principles, and that in the end, He will just give us the ice cream.

News flash, He won't.

The Lord, Jesus said in Matthew 6:33, "But seek ye first the kingdom of God, and His righteousness; and all these things shall be added unto you." People like this verse, but there is an entire chapter full of verses before this one. In fact, there are 32 verses. He promises to provide food and clothing, but it's conditional. We must seek Him first. According to Christ, if we don't seek righteous living and put God in first place, then we have no promise of God doing what He said He would do.

In Africa, God directed my path. He met all of my needs, and I did not go without. I learned that God is faithful, and I can trust Him to take care of me. Even when I am in a strange land, completely ignorant of my surroundings, God will take care of me.

It still amazes me that Proverbs 3:5-6, a verse I memorized as a child and carried with me all my life, was used by the Lord to teach me in Africa. What I discovered in a great and exciting way was that God keeps His word, and His promises are true. This verse became a precious reality to this poor servant.

Would I do it again?

After all the craziness of the trip, people have often asked me this question. My response?

"Yes! In a heartbeat."

I went back the following year. And in March, we made another trip and had a great time. On that trip, everything went smoothly with no hiccups.

God is always faithful. All He asks is that we trust Him and believe His word.

NOTES

"Stuff." Def. 8. *AV1611.com.* <u>AV1611, 2019. Web. 1 April 2019.</u>

ABOUT THE AUTHOR

Matthew B Swiatkowski Sr. was born and raised in Kearny, NJ. He trusted Jesus Christ as his personal Saviour at the age of ten, and in 1982, as a senior in high school, he surrendered his life to serve the Lord. He was a youth pastor and assistant pastor of Gospel Light Baptist Church in Kearny until he was called to be the head pastor in 1995, and he continues to serve there to this day.

Matthew is married to his college sweetheart, Ann Renee. They have been blessed with four children, two of whom are married. At present, they have two grandchildren.

ACKNOWLEDGMENTS

The writing of this book would not have been possible were it not for the following people.

Lee and Peggy Weaver who first started going to Sierra Leone to help the people by drilling wells for water and doing nursing work. It was this dear couple who introduced this ministry to David Arnold. Only eternity will tell the true story of their love and sacrifice. They are true servants and lovers of people everywhere.

Dr. David Arnold who has done an incredible work in helping Africa through his mission, World Evangelistic Outreach. Not only has he tirelessly traveled America's roads to visit churches to raise support for the work in Sierra Leone, but he has also traveled to Africa every year, and on many occasions, several times a year. I can tell you honestly that he truly loves the country and its people.

Max Gorvie, now home with the Lord, worked tirelessly to reach Africans with the Gospel of Jesus Christ. He was up long before dawn in order to pray and read his Bible, and on many occasions, he walked for miles to reach the next village. He left a godly legacy for his children and others to follow.

To Solomon Gorvie for being a friend to a man he had never met before and the amazing work he performs. I am humbled by the work he does and the heavy responsibility he carries.

To all the pastors, church workers, school principals, teachers, and lay people in Sierra Leonne and Liberia. I dare not mention names for the fear that I may leave someone out. They labor in intense heat, little comfort, have inadequate supplies, are under paid, and for many, did this work while a war around them raged. I am humbled by them all. I fully expect to be positioned behind them when we stand at the Bema Judgement seat.

For the people of our church here at Gospel Light Baptist and my friends. You made it possible for me to be part of this trip with your sacrificial giving and love. I love you all and thank you.

To my wife, Renee, who loves me and prayed for me the whole time I was gone on this trip. It was her prayers and concern that encouraged me the most. She stayed home and held the fort down while I was on my big adventure. Someday, Lord willing, we will go together.

To my friend, Dr. Don Woodard, who, when I told him I had written a book but was uneasy about publishing it, encouraged me and pushed me forward.

A special thank you to Trisha Longmire for her hard work in editing this manuscript.

And to the wonderful people at Ambassador International who have been kind and gracious through this entire process.

For more information about

Matthew B. Swiatkowski Sr.

and

Africa: My First Missions Trip . . . What Could Go Wrong?

please visit:
www.gospellightbaptistchurch.net
www.facebook.com/GLBCNJ

www.ambassador-international.com
@AmbassadorIntl
www.facebook.com/AmbassadorIntl

If you enjoyed this book, please consider leaving us a review on Amazon, Goodreads, or our website.